The +10 Percent Principle

How to Get Extraordinary Results from Ordinary People

The +10 Percent Principle

How to Get Extraordinary Results from Ordinary People

Barrie Richardson With
Mary Ann Castronovo Fusco

Pfeiffer
& COMPANY

Amsterdam • Johannesburg • London
San Diego • Sydney • Toronto

Published by:
Pfeiffer & Company
8517 Production Avenue
San Diego, California 92121-2280 USA

Library of Congress Cataloging-in-Publication Data
Richardson, Barrie.
    The +10 percent principle: how to get extraordinary results from
    ordinary people/ Barrie Richardson, Mary Ann Fusco.
      p. cm.
    ISBN 0-88390-371-7 — ISBN 0-89384-221-4 (pbk.)
    1. Management—United States. 2. Leadership—United States.
I. Fucso, Mary Ann. II. Title. III. Title: Plus ten% principle.
IV. Title: Plus 10 percent principle.
HD31.R493 1993   92-51045
658.4'092–dc20   CIP

Printed in the United States of America.
Printing 1 2 3 4 5 6 7 8 9 10

Printed on acid-free, recycled stock that meets or exceeds
the minimum GPO and EPA specifications for recycled paper.

Dedication

To four remarkable persons—Craig, Jan, Pam, and David Richardson.

—Barrie Richardson

To my extraordinary parents, Rosario and Paola Castronovo, who give 110 percent in everything they do.

—Mary Ann Castronovo Fusco

Contents

Acknowledgments

Many thanks to those at Centenary College of Louisiana who helped in the preparation of the manuscript for this book, especially Marcy Frantom and Pat Briffa for their excellent typing job, and Christy Wrenn for her meticulous library research. A final word of appreciation goes to Lyle Steele of Lyle Steele & Company, New York City, for his persistence and dedication to this project.

–B.R. and M.C.F.

Introduction

Can you name five extraordinary organizations? Maybe several names easily come to mind. But most people have a hard time completing the list. After some discussion, participants in my management workshops generally come up with such organizations as Wal-Mart, Alcoholics Anonymous, the Boston Celtics, Nordstrom, and DisneyWorld. Rarely do they mention their church, a local supermarket, or the place where they work.

The fact is, we all are members of several organizations, and we have contact with dozens of others each day; yet few of them are truly outstanding.

The performance of most organizations—schools, retail shops, volunteer groups, churches, manufacturing firms—fluctuates somewhere between mediocre and satisfactory. Why is this? What can be done to transform ordinary organizations into extraordinary ones?

The +10 Percent Principle answers this question. This book presents simple but powerful concepts that can help anyone boost the performance of their organization—be it a business, school, union, government agency, church, orchestra, volunteer group, or athletic team.

What Makes The +10 Percent Principle *Different?*

Unlike many other books on leadership and management, *The +10 Percent Principle* is not academic or theoretical. It offers no scholarly reports or studies, no tables, graphs, or charts. This book has grown out of my experience as a consultant, teacher, and manager. The concepts and ideas that are discussed within these pages are not arid theories, but are taken from real-life events. And these ideas are presented through the use of anecdotes, parables, and metaphors. No, this is not a typical approach, but after nearly thirty years of teaching college students and managers in the United States and Great Britain, I've come to realize how important it is to make ideas come alive. I know that this is how I learn best. And apparently, so do most people.

For example, one May morning, Walter Grammer, the manager of a department store in Little Rock, Arkansas, invited me to speak to his company's employees.

"Barrie," he said, "I would like you to talk about 'the +10 percent principle,' 'the Chinese eye,' and 'the mental midgets.'"

"Wait," I said. "How do you remember those concepts? Did you take notes or have me taped when I talked to your corporate officers?"

"No, I just remember them," he replied.

A few hours later, Bryan Hall, the president of Five Star Financial Services, called from Valencia, California.

"Do you think you can come to our retreat in Houston and lead a seminar for corporate managers and our licensees?" he asked. "I would like you to talk about 'the invisible foundations of Salisbury,' 'the redwoods,' and 'the Easter Island stones.' Do you think you can also demonstrate how we all say 'no' too soon to things that we think are impossible but that we really can do?"

"How did you remember those ideas?" I asked.

"Everyone remembers them," he answered. "They're simple and dynamic."

Kelly Michaels, a recent graduate, stopped by that afternoon.

"Now that your management course is over, I can tell you I will never forget the metaphors, especially 'the quaking aspens' and 'the listening lever,'" she said.

Metaphors like the ones in the chapters that follow conjure pictures in our minds that help us cut through to the heart of what originally seemed to be a complicated matter or concept. And that, I think, is what makes them so universally appealing. Parables and anecdotes have been used by teachers since the time of Aesop. They worked then, they work today.

The Journey From Ordinary to Extraordinary

The central theme of *The +10 Percent Principle* is that although each one of us is gifted with creative and intellectual capacities, we usually are not called on to fully use them. Successful organizations, however, have one thing in common: Their leaders—be they managers, coaches, teachers, or ministers—establish an environment in which ordinary people are encouraged to give their best effort.

Chapter 1: From Ordinary to Extraordinary presents a simple but potent idea: The difference between being ordinary and extraordinary in most organizations—basketball teams and banks, orchestras and restaurants, schools and offices, hospitals and factories—is not a huge increment, but only a small amount—10 percent.

This one insight has had a great impact on hundreds, maybe thousands, of persons I've met over the years. It can galvanize a group to reach higher—to become extraordinary.

Chapter 2: Your Amazing Mind explains how most of us tend to depreciate our own abilities. We stand in awe of computers and marvel at the workmanship of beavers and birds. Yet no other animal and no machine can approach us in our capacity to adapt, communicate, and innovate. This means that the average person is, in fact, gifted.

Chapter 3: What's Holding Us Back? asks the question, "Why is it that ordinary people like you and me who have Porsche mental motors perform like 1978 Fiestas?" This section reveals the limitations we place on ourselves and the role our environment plays in helping us reach our full potential—or in keeping us from doing so.

Chapter 4: The +10 Percent Team shows how leaders often curb productive thinking and demotivate team members rather than release their creativity. Individuals form groups, or teams, to multiply their strengths, but most fall far short of their potential. This chapter explains how to turn that around.

Chapter 5: Ideas That Work stresses that good intentions are not enough. There are practical skills and concepts that leaders must use. Deceptively simple, most of these ideas do not appear in any textbook, but they're here.

Chapter 6: Catalytic Leadership shows that leadership is not the same as management. Many organizations are well run, but few are superb. Leadership is like yeast—it lifts the organization. Leaders need vision, moral courage, and a passionate persistence—not charisma.

Chapter 7: The +10 Percent Principle in Action uses case studies to illustrate the fact that high-performing organizations have a great deal in common. They enter the winner's circle not by superhuman achievement, but by doing 10 percent better in significant areas. All the organizations described in this chapter create an environment in which ordinary people are committed to giving their best.

Chapter 8: Managing by Metaphor wraps up everything we've learned in the preceding chapters. Why is it that we remember stories that we were told as children or a parable we heard in church? Management metaphors also seem to stick in our minds and can be retrieved when we need them. Leaders need to find metaphors that summarize their goals, aspirations, and philosophy.

This book can be read in two ways. For example, you can choose any essay in the book and be able to glean a message from it. I have a minister friend, Don McDowell, who has used many of these ideas in his sermons. Another friend, Ed Markovich, a financial advisor, shares selected essays with his associates. School teachers, coaches, social workers, and hospital administrators have all found several of these essays helpful in their work.

Most readers, however, probably will find it more useful to read through each chapter and think about and, perhaps, even discuss the ideas presented in it before moving on. You can think of this book as a travel guide. There's a daily travel schedule and a final destination. You can follow this guidebook chapter by chapter, or you can go to any spot you like and ignore the schedule and ultimate destination.

Whichever method you choose, *The +10 Percent Principle* should be fun to read. You will find many of the stories it contains both provocative and memorable. Easter Island idols, the Sears Tower, Cardini the Magician, firewalkers, dwarfs, Salisbury Cathedral, redwood trees, and all sorts of seemingly diverse people, places, and events will be used to illustrate many ideas.

At the end of the book you will be pleasantly surprised to see that you remember the concepts you've read about—not because you studied them, but because the examples and stories are so vivid that you can't forget them. You will find that not only will you recall these ideas when you are invited to do so in the last chapter, but you also will use these ideas in your daily personal and professional life.

With that said, let's start our trip.

1

From Ordinary to Extraordinary

How can mediocre organizations be transformed into extraordinary organizations? What does it mean to be extraordinary? Are there principles, concepts, or guidelines that can be used to get extraordinary performance from ordinary people? What does it take to do common things uncommonly well?

Leaders of outstanding organizations in any field of human endeavor seem to share many values and principles. For one thing, they don't use complicated, abstruse, or theoretical techniques. Rather, they rely on simple, practical concepts. These deceptively simple ideas, like the ideas contained in the "Sermon on the Mount" or the *Bhagavad-Gita*, are easy to comprehend, but not always easy to put into action.

An idea can be simple and yet not be simplistic. The Jaguar has simple yet elegant lines. Einstein's theory of general relativity is summarized in a simple statement. Adam Smith's metaphor of people who follow their own self-interest as if they were led by an invisible hand to serve

1

the common good is both a simple and a brilliant insight that captures the essence of how the free market works.

The +10 Percent Principle

The single most meaningful management principle I know isn't found in any of the traditional textbooks on management. I call this simple but powerful concept "the +10 Percent Principle."

This principle, which can have an immediate and also profound impact on both organizations and individuals, can certainly be used by first-line supervisors, sales managers, newspaper editors, hospital administrators, and top-level executives. It also can be used by high-school principals, ministers, university presidents, athletic coaches, government leaders, teachers, choir conductors, and anyone else who is interested in high performance. An insight into how the world operates, this concept can affect quality, productivity, sales, profits, and morale by galvanizing and energizing ordinary people to perform at extraordinary levels.

The crucial point of this principle is that the difference between ordinary and extraordinary in most human organizations—basketball teams, banks, orchestras, restaurants, and schools—is of a vastly different magnitude than that which we find in other areas of the world.

Have you ever seen Mt. Ranier from a boat on Puget Sound? If you have, it will not take long to recall the sight because it is so spectacular that it's unforgettable. Like a giant Buddha, Mt. Ranier looms over the whole city of Seattle. Although the other mountains in this range are tall and majestic in their own right, Mt. Ranier's considerable height and girth make them seem puny by comparison.

Have you ever been in the viewing gallery of the 110-story-high Sears Tower in Chicago? From there, on a clear day, you can see for 30 or 40 miles. When you look at the city below, you get the feeling that you're looking at miniatures. Even skyscrapers like the IBM Plaza and the Lincoln Tower look like small toys. Yet, when you stand on Michigan Avenue or LaSalle Street and look up, these very same office buildings look enormous.

The difference between Mt. Ranier and the other mountains in its range or between the Sears Tower and the other Chicago skyscrapers is not modest but immense. Ordinary versus extraordinary in both these examples is a huge and dramatic differential.

In almost all human organizations, however, the difference between what we call outstanding and pedestrian is nothing like the differential between the Sears Tower and the Lincoln Tower. In fact, the difference between being a run-of-the-mill organization and a high-performing one is a small increment. This increment is the cornerstone of the +10 Percent Principle. Of course, 10 percent is neither a literal concept nor necessarily even a quantitative measure. Rather, it is a metaphor for the surprisingly small gap between those who stand in the winner's circle and the also-rans.

Take Joe Namath for example. In 1966 he was the highest-paid quarterback in the American Football League and his performance, both on and off the field, was front-page news. He clearly was a winner.

But how much better than the average was Broadway Joe's performance? Was his pass-completion rate 50 percent better? No. Was it 20 percent better than the league's average rate? No. A mere 6.5 percent made Namath a standout. Think about it. This 6.5 percent superior performance over the *average* quarterback, not the quarterback who was second in pass completions, made Joe Namath a phenomenon.

How often do you come across a really outstanding organization? Reflect on your own experiences over the last few days. Would you give an "A+" rating to your supermarket, auto shop, beauty salon, bank, or department store? What about your church or your children's school? Now think about the place where you work. Most of us work for organizations that produce average products or deliver average services and earn average rates of return for their investors. Most of us receive an average wage for an average day's work. If we are really honest, most of us would say that most organizations we deal with are acceptable. On balance, they deliver satisfactory products and services. Few are outstanding.

But if, as the +10 Percent Principle shows, the difference between being one of a select cadre of high performers and being quite average is small, then modest improvements can have remarkable results. The +10 Percent Principle, then, can be used as a management tool to improve organizations in all walks of life.

Over the last 10 years, I've talked with groups of nurses, teachers, supervisors, managers, salespeople, engineers, technicians, secretaries, social workers, and government employees. I asked them, "How many of you want to be part of an outstanding organization?" Almost everyone raised their hands. Then I asked, "How many of you have the know-how to reduce costs and improve quality in your department by an extra 10 percent?" Consistently, 90 percent of the people in the audience raised their hands again.

What if every teacher on a high-school faculty decided to improve just one course by 10 percent next year? What if a city police force found ways to reduce not all crimes, but violent crimes, by 10 percent? What if a hospital could reduce lab costs by 10 percent? What if a national pharmaceutical company could cut the lead time on significant products by 10 percent? Or, what if every married person made a commitment to spend 10 percent more time listening to his or her spouse?

One good way to understand the process and power of small change is to see how most of us behave when given choices. How many of you would consider going to a new bakery if it sold freshly baked goods that were 10 percent better in quality than those sold where you usually shop? What if the salespeople in this new bakery were polite, called you by name, and carefully and quickly packed each item in a cardboard box rather than tossing them into a paper sack? Would you change hairdressers or barbers if you felt you would get a 10 percent better haircut? Would you pay 30 percent more to be 10 percent more attractive? What about automobile repair, banking, or dry cleaning? Would you change vendors for a 10 percent differential? Would you consider trying a new stockbroker if he or she could give you 10 percent better returns, or change physicians for 10 percent better treatment? Would you pay a premium tuition to a private school if the faculty there could improve the competence and self-confidence of your children by 10 percent over the local public school?

The +10 Percent Principle doesn't require everyone to change their allegiance to stores, banks, or schools because of a perceived small differential in quality or service. But even a 10 percent switch makes a major difference. What would be the consequences if a dry cleaning shop, for example, lost 10 percent of its business? Overhead costs would remain the same, but the owner's income would suffer. On the other hand, what would happen if there were a 10 percent increase in business? Most firms can easily handle 10 percent more customers, and this 10 percent increase can generate a 50 percent or greater increase in profit. In both cases, just an extra 10 percent change in revenue can have immediate and dramatic consequences.

This concept becomes even more powerful when we combine it with the principle of the vital few. Vilfredo Pareto, a turn-of-the-century Italian economist and sociologist, discovered that for most manufacturing firms a small number of inventory items, less than 10 percent, accounted for 90 percent of the total value of their inventory. This holds true for our personal balance sheets. Most of us own hundreds of things—clothes, books, records— but our homes, cars, and savings may account for 90 percent of our net worth. The idea that a few items or events, the vital few, have a major impact on results is a potent concept.

An organization, then, does not need to be better at everything to be outstanding; it only needs to be better at the vital few. Marriott, for example, one of the most admired companies in the hotel industry, has outdistanced its competition by being better in one vital area, customer service. Middlebury College in Vermont is a fine liberal arts college, but it has earned a special reputation for its language programs. Federal Express has emphasized time—absolutely, positively overnight delivery—to ensure success. What if two supermarkets, both conveniently located, sold the same kinds of goods at about the same prices? What would you do if one of the stores had fruit and vegetables (its vital few) that were 10 percent better than its competitor's?

The +10 Percent Principle also can apply to costs. What would happen if an organization could find a way to reduce costs by 10 percent? What would be the impact on profits, employee bonuses, or research and development if there were a 10 percent reduction in costs? In 1983, AT&T took 22 days to manufacture a telephone. By focusing on a few vital areas of manufacturing, the company cut that time down to 58 minutes. Similarly, a 10 percent reduction in an organization's inventory can have a huge impact: Plant size is smaller, utility costs fall, and emphasis is placed on doing things right the first time.

So what's keeping organizations from performing at higher levels? Is it lazy, greedy workers? Do high-performing organizations hire only people who are highly disciplined and self-motivated? Do their employees have extraordinary capacities?

Yes, they do hire people with good work habits, but most of their employees are ordinary people like you and me. What these high-performing organizations do is create an environment in which ordinary people voluntarily choose to give their best physical, intellectual, and creative efforts to the goals of the organization.

Most organizations hover between mediocre and satisfactory performance because their managers don't know how to release and direct the energies of ordinary people. Nor do they know how to teach them to work as a team that's motivated, not out of fear or by bribes, but because it feels it is involved in doing something worthy and it wants to do it well.

Most people—coaches, principals, supervisors—seem to be satisfied with mediocrity even though they probably would describe themselves as above-average individuals leading above-average organizations. Those who realize that high performance is within everyone's reach can lift their group's vision and ignite the imagination and determination of everyone around them to be first-rate.

Lessons From the Derby

Do you know the jockey who rode a 17-to-1 longshot to victory in the 1986 Kentucky Derby?

Chances are that you do. Bill Shoemaker's stunning feat made for one of the most memorable races in the history of Derby competition. But what you may not have realized is that there are four powerful management lessons that can be drawn from this story of a 54-year-old jockey entering the winner's circle astride a 3-year-old colt trained by a 73-year-old man.

Lesson 1: You've Got to Believe

Shoemaker is not a boastful man. When he went on record 2 weeks before the Derby saying, "Mark my words, this horse [Ferdinand] will win the Derby," he meant it.

High-performing organizations need leaders who believe in the strengths of those in their group. Teams exist to multiply the strengths of individuals, but the leader must be able to visualize victory and articulate it to others. Shoemaker believed in the trainer, the horse, and himself, and that belief led to his victory.

Here is another example of the power of believing. While riding on a Chicago subway some time ago, I overheard a young man talking to a friend about his dream of becoming a world-famous performer within the next 5 years. That night in the theater, I saw the same man portraying a magician in *The Magic Man*, a facsimile of the long-running New York success, *The Magic Show*, starring Doug Henning. The Chicago play was not memorable, but the 19-year-old performer, who at that time had only modest technical competence in magic, was positively magnetic. Before he had turned 21, he had a national reputation, and by age 24, he had done two television specials. He is now considered one of the premier magicians in the world. David Copperfield saw himself clearly in the role he wanted to play, and he grew into it.

Conversely, *not* believing in yourself can be dangerous. Take the case of Karl Wallenda, founder of the famous Flying Wallendas high-wire acrobats. He once said that being on the tightrope was living, and everything else was waiting. But on March 22, 1978, in San Juan, Puerto Rico, Karl Wallenda fell 75 feet to his death. According to his wife, before his performance that day and for the first time in his career, Wallenda saw himself falling, not succeeding, in his dreams. He checked and double-checked the wires and support struts, which he rarely did, and he told others how his upcoming tightrope walk spooked him. Wallenda previously had seen himself as being successful. On that fateful day in 1978, however, he was concentrating on *not falling*, rather than focusing on succeeding. Do you see yourself and your team as winners?

Lesson 2: Encouragement Beats Whipping

When the horses in the 1986 Derby broke from the gate, there was bumping and some confusion. Ferdinand was dead last in the field of sixteen, and a half mile into the race he was at the back of the pack.

Did Shoemaker apply the whip? No. The horse under him wanted to run, and Shoemaker knew it, so he coached him on with a firm but gentle grip. On the far turn Shoemaker made his move, passing horses on the outside until he was positioned fifth coming into the home stretch.

The average worker yearns to be a hero, if only for a short time. Most of us, whether we are clerks, clergymen, or secretaries, want to run a good race. Survey after survey has shown that managers, and those they manage, want two things from their job: (1) a challenging assignment with a lot of stretch, and (2) self-control in doing their assignment. But too many managers believe that only the whip—coercion, imposed controls, and penalties—will yield high performance. In fact, however, increasing penalties and the number of controls reduces quality, productivity, and morale. Do you have a firm but gentle grip?

Lesson 3: Don't Mistake Resistance for Limits

As Ferdinand came into the homestretch, four horses were ahead of him. The easiest path to take was to go around the wall of horses. Shoemaker saw a hole open on his left and boldly chose to go right through the center of those thoroughbreds. Ferdinand accelerated and burst through, passing all the horses and running away with the race.

Increased effort generally is needed for increased results. This is the universal law of nature that economists call the law of diminishing returns. As we attempt to get more output—sales from a given territory, wheat from a farm, or juice from an orange—we require ever increasing amounts of effort to get smaller and smaller returns. But the law does not hold up when we find a new or better way of doing whatever it is that we are doing.

We often mistake resistance for limits. But sometimes we can break through to a new height of achievement by following what looks like the line of greatest, not least, resistance.

Lesson 4: Small Increments Can Take You Far

Although Ferdinand started last, Shoemaker was able to get him to pass ten horses on the track, and then he skillfully guided him through a hole in the traffic at the top of the homestretch to win by 2¼ lengths.

Do you know the name of the English colt that came in second on that memorable day in May? What about his jockey's name? Probably not. Yet, the difference between first and second place is only a small margin. This race was 1¼ miles long. The difference between the first and second horse (Bold Arrangement) was 20 feet, or one second on the clock. The difference between the average time and Ferdinand's time in this race was only a few seconds. What would have happened if Ferdinand had had a clean start?

And so it is in life. The difference between those who stand out in almost any field of human performance—music, sales, journalism, investments, surgery—and the rest of the field is a small margin. Just think about it. How much taller is a person who stands head and shoulders above everyone else? Just 10 percent will do it. A salesperson who closes 10 percent more sales, a stockbroker who does 10 percent better than the average, or a college that gets a 10 percent higher performance from its students, will have a long line of people gladly paying for their services. Who would not be willing to pay a premium for a 10 percent improvement in quality or service of a product, or a 10 percent higher return on their money? Yet, if only 10 percent of the market turns to this above-average supplier, there will be a powerful multiplier effect on its profits. Such is the power of small increments.

Four powerful and durable management lessons are learned from the 112th Kentucky Derby. They are easy to understand, but all too often they are not put into practice. The minority who do apply them are easy to spot: They're on their way to or already in the winner's circle.

Elegant Principles

An elegant principle is one that does a lot with a little. There is great pleasure in discovering a lean, clean, and simple solution to a problem. When our minds restructure a situation and perceive a simple yet powerful solution, the surprise of finding the answer delights us. Much like when a paradox or a magic trick that at first stumps us but then, once explained, seems so obvious, when we finally come to a solution after much thought, it seems so easy and self-evident.

If I asked you to determine how many basketball games would have to be played in a single elimination tournament if fifteen teams signed up for the event, you could, no doubt, figure it out. Most of us would draw a tree-like diagram and note that in the first round one team would have a bye. Eventually, we would end up with fourteen matches and a winner.

This is a perfectly good way to solve this problem. But there are others. For example, you might have a computer software program do these calculations for you in a few seconds, or you might work the problem inductively and find a recursive principle at work, or you could use algebra to find the solution.

But there is an entirely different way of solving this problem without using computers, mathematical formulas, or tree diagrams. Furthermore, this method will provide you with the answer not only for this example, but for all problems like this. And best of all, you can do it in your head in seconds.

Rather than focusing on the mathematics, let's look at the logic. In any single elimination tournament, there can be only one winner. Right? In our example, we would have one winner and fourteen losers. Now look at the losers. How many games does it take to make one loser? One game, of course. And fourteen losers would take fourteen games. Therefore, since each loss requires one game, we need to schedule fourteen games. See how we have restructured the problem by changing our focus?

Now watch the power of this simple solution in action. How many tennis matches would you have to schedule if ninety-seven people entered a single elimination tournament? A minute ago you may have shaken your head and groaned. Now the answer is so easy: ninety-six. What we have here is an elegant principle—it does a lot with a little.

The idea of brilliant simplicity is not limited to science or mathematics or magic. We find the same idea in art, architecture, music, and in the management of organizations. After more than 25 years of experience, I still continue to be surprised and delighted when I discover simple but powerful principles at work in the marketplace. And I grow more and more convinced that the complicated and abstruse management models and theories that are generated and taught in graduate schools of business miss the mark. They frequently can't be put into practice, conflict with real world events, and ignore an important fact: Management innovators rarely think in terms of complex equations; rather, they tend to use common-sense principles.

Have you heard of a British firm called John Lewis Partnership? This organization operates under the same basic philosophy that John Lewis, its founder, put in place in 1864: *We will never be undersold.* Now a large retail organization that owns a chain of department stores and supermarkets, John Lewis Partnership expects each salesperson to treat every customer as they would their own mother. *Total commitment to value and quality* is the company's motto.

John Lewis Partnership has never spent money on paid advertising. Can you imagine a supermarket with no newspaper ads or special sales posted in the window? Can you imagine a department store closing on Saturday afternoons so employees can spend time with their families? Can you imagine a giant merchandising firm that uses a simple color-coded card system for inventory control? Can you imagine a business that shares all sales information with every employee each week? Can you imagine a firm that allows the employees themselves to recommend, after a year's trial, who will be given permanent status and participate in profit-sharing?

If this seems like a strange place to you, think again. John Lewis Partnership is consistently one of the most profitable retail chains in Europe. Its employees receive annual bonuses equal to 20 percent of their salaries, the employee turnover rate is low, and employee morale is high—all because of the application of simple concepts, powerful concepts, elegant concepts.

Almost everyone knows that Japan is the world's largest producer of automobiles. But few people outside the auto industry realize that under the leadership of a former machinist, Taiichi Ohno, a revolutionary method of production, the Toyota Production System, evolved over three decades. This system not only produces autos at two-thirds the cost of cars in the United States or Europe, it also produces some of the most dependable cars in the world.

The Toyota *just-in-time* (JIT) concept eliminates the need for inventory and warehouses. Each manufacturing component arrives at the right place at the right time in flawless condition. A kanban, an information-carrying colored card, travels the production line with the components, and tells workers when to order new parts. Here is a simple, nontechnological concept that has revolutionized production. Expecting to see space-age technology, visitors to the Toyota plant are surprised to see how conventional the operations appear and are impressed with how tidy, clean, and quiet the factory is.

The basic idea for this production system came to Kiichiri Toyoda when he visited an American supermarket in 1935. He noted how fresh fruit and vegetables were always in stock; yet, there were no large warehouses on the premises. This simple and powerful idea gave rise to the Toyota Production System, a system whose two legs are *respect for people* and the *elimination of waste*.

But we need not travel to England or Japan to find elegant management thinking. For example, Sam Walton's concepts of merchandising, purchasing, and transporting made him one of the richest men in the world in less than 30 years. And now his idea of deep discounting in a warehouse environment has further propelled his company.

Management expert Peter Drucker has noted that for an innovation to be effective it has to be simple and focused. If not, it will not work. He asserts that all effective innovations are breathtakingly simple—in short, elegant.

The Merrill Lynch Cash Management Account (CMA) is such an idea. There are scores of clones, but Merrill Lynch has over 50 percent of the business. Why didn't banks, or insurance firms, or other investment firms come up with the simple and powerful idea of managing cash for middle-income people in the way corporations handle their cash? Why didn't I think of it? It seems so easy.

On a smaller scale, there are powerful, elegant lessons to be learned from John Porter, who runs a dry-cleaning business with his family.

Almost anyone can get into this business, which requires no specialized training or capital. You would think that in such a competitive, open environment, all dry cleaners would make an ordinary rate of return. On balance, this is true. But Porter's Cleaners is not a typical dry cleaner. John Porter and his team have one of the most successful dry-cleaning operations in the country. What's going on?

Porter doesn't offer special discounts or two-for-one promotions. Price is not the attraction here. Neither is location. In fact, many customers go miles out of their way to do business with him. What complicated, sophisticated management ideas are behind his operation? None!

John Porter is brilliant in the basics. After college and before starting his dry-cleaning venture, he sold carpets. That is when he learned some vital lessons in superior customer service.

Porter is not a technician. Unlike many people in his industry, he didn't focus his energies on learning how to mix chemicals, fix equipment, or take stains out of ties. He hired the best people he could find to do this. Porter's eye was and is on the customer. How could he reduce the hassles customers have and add value to his services? That was the challenge he set out to tackle.

He introduced several innovations. First, his customers don't have to leave their vehicles. A well-dressed college student greets customers at their cars when they pull into the parking area. The customers indicate when they would like to pick up their clean garments. There are no receipts that would slow down the process. When the customers return, a friendly person greets them, asks their name, and in a few seconds returns and then hangs the clean clothing in their car. Small repairs—buttons sewn on, a torn cuff mended—are made without being requested. John Porter spends 5 percent of his revenue supporting cultural events and community charities and on advertising. Everything his company does smacks of quality.

Yet anyone can do these things. The real secret to Porter's success is the way he delivers his services. Employees are carefully selected and trained to be enthusiastic and polite. They consistently do a good job. They offer reimbursement for a damaged garment on the spot, no disputes. They ask for complaints, and when things go astray, they generally manage to convert the unhappy customer into a joyful one. They treat every client as though he or she were the single most important customer.

Competence, consistency, enthusiasm, and courtesy—sounds simple, doesn't it? Porter's management principles are quite simple, elegantly simple. There are other elegant principles waiting to be perceived and conceived where you live and work.

2

Your Amazing Mind

You are not faster than a speeding bullet or more powerful than a locomotive. Superman you are not. But you are amazing. I often ask participants in my management workshops to raise their right hand if they think they have an incredible mind. They generally smile and chuckle, and ultimately only a few brave people lift their hands. But the unvarnished fact is this: Each one of us has extraordinary capacities.

I'm not talking about paranormal capacities, such as telepathy, precognition, or psychokinesis; nor am I referring to genius-level performance. Indeed, we have a tendency to romanticize the capacities of such people as Mozart, Newton, and Einstein and to greatly understate our own capabilities. We also try to gauge our abilities by comparing them to the performance of computers. But we are not machines. So it's no wonder that when we compare our calculating ability with that of a computer, we come up short. We also tend to attribute special capacities to lower animals—capacities that they probably do not have.

Yes, you and I are animals, but we can do things that no porpoise—or computer, for that matter—can do. The gift of every so-called ordinary person is perception. We can see things in our mind's eye. How we take in information, sort it out, store it, and retrieve it, is still largely a mystery.

What's not a mystery is the fact that our species is not bounded by evolution or environment the way monkeys and whales are. In what must be a mere wink in terms of geological time, we have gone from being hunters and gatherers to being the superior species on earth. We are not angels. We may pollute the earth beyond repair or blow it up, but there's no question that we stand apart from all other animals.

I once asked a group of production managers to draw a picture of their minds. The pictures were then taped on a wall. The one we labeled as best that day was of an iceberg. Most of the participants agreed that each of us uses a small fraction of our capacity. Like an iceberg, 80 to 90 percent of our potential is hidden.

During the management training program on my first job after college three decades ago, a plant manager told me that his people were M & Ms—mental midgets who needed to be told exactly what to do.

How do you view your capacities? Do you denigrate your abilities? Do you use your imagination to find your faults and those of others? How do you look upon the abilities of so-called average people?

Leaders need to start with themselves. The average person is a gifted person. Once we understand the immensity of our own capacity and the power of our imagination, then we're ready to lead. Ordinary people can do extraordinary things when leaders help them release their talents and abilities, and direct these creative skills toward productive activities.

Let's start with our amazing minds by examining how our brains function. In this chapter we'll find out why we can say we have Porsche mental motors. Mental midgets? Never!

Seeing With the Chinese Eye

Put your hand out, palm up. Now imagine that there's a 6-inch-tall man standing in your palm. Pull off one of his arms. Ugh! Now pull off the other. Throw them away. Now bend him back and forth at the middle until his body breaks off at the waist. Throw the upper half away. Next, imagine putting a two-inch eye on top of the remaining torso.

Carefully pick up this strange little creature, basically an eye atop two legs, and place it in your pocket or purse. Congratulations! You now have a wonderful gift that you can take out and use any time you want. What you have is a permanent reminder that there's another way of seeing—an oriental way of seeing—that will help your mind break free from limited perspectives that stifle its creativity.

As you probably know, written Chinese uses thousands of characters, pictographs, to communicate ideas. The pictograph for seeing is not just an eye, but an open eye atop two legs.

Why is the eye on legs? Well, what can an eye with legs do that an eye can't do fixed in one place? The Chinese eye is a metaphor for walking around situations, looking at them from inside or outside, top or bottom, up close or from afar. For thousands of years the Chinese have known that people with fixed vision become inflexible and intolerant thinkers. They believe there's a more flexible and fluid way to view reality.

Magicians know how to fool spectators' eyes; so does Mother Nature. Have you ever watched the sun slowly sink over a body of water? Sunsets can stir the soul. But if you could look at the same sunset from a distant space station, you'd see that the sun isn't setting at all; rather, the earth is turning on its axis. Intellectually we know this, but we don't see it that way.

Often we fool ourselves. We like the world to be tidy and well-ordered. But most creative achievements have come from people who have looked at situations with a Chinese eye. Rather than seeing what is clear and obvious, they have walked around a situation and developed a novel, and sometimes revolutionary, perspective.

Great scientists such as Newton, Mendel, and Einstein looked at the existing world differently, with a Chinese eye, and produced elegant and powerful models of how the physical world behaves. Creative artists such as Bach, Dali, and Melville also used the Chinese-eye approach to produce great works of art.

Yet, the gift of the Chinese eye is not available only to scientists and artists. The capacity to break out of the conventional mode and see things differently belongs to everyone. In fact, most of the stimulation, joy, and comfort we enjoy today has come from billions of small improvements made by millions of largely unremarkable people.

Robert Cope, an engineer and expert on Japanese manufacturing, tells a story about overhearing an interesting conversation in a hotel lobby in Grand Rapids, Michigan, in 1982. One automotive engineer was asking another if he had heard the wild story of how Toyota supposedly could change the stamping die used for one fender to a die needed to stamp the other fender in 15 minutes. The engineers were skeptical, since the die-changing time in the United States was 6 hours. But the engineer's information was wrong. In 1982, the actual Japanese time was 12 minutes. And still they were not happy. Their die-changing time fell to 2 minutes, and now it is only a few seconds' delay. Impossible? Not if one sees with a Chinese eye. Today, some American auto manufacturers can produce the last car of one model year and then turn out the first car of the following model year without stopping the production line.

Wal-Mart is one of the great commercial success stories of the twentieth century. What enabled Sam Walton, a small-town Arkansas merchant, to become one of the richest men in the world in two decades? The answer is neither family wealth nor political clout; neither luck nor hard work alone. The answer is the Chinese eye.

Sam Walton looked at retailing differently than his competitors did. He saw an opportunity to serve a market that others saw as too small. Wal-Mart initially didn't make its name in big cities, but in small towns of under 5,000 people. Walton also looked at pricing, merchandise quality, and use of retail employees with a fresh eye. He coordinated physical storage and distribution in a way that has not been equaled. Sam Walton succeeded because he, just like many others before and after him, viewed his world through a Chinese eye.

Supermarkets, which are still slow in coming to much of Europe, were started by Michael "King" Kullen in Jamaica, New York, in 1930. Why didn't A&P, the master of food merchandising back then, see the possibility?

Federal Express will deliver packages overnight. Why didn't others see the need for this service first?

The rigid mind can come up with dozens of reasons why a particular venture is impossible or impractical. But now that you possess that special creature with the open eye atop two legs, you, too, can view the world and all its opportunities with a Chinese eye. It's a gift that truly makes you gifted.

Don't Jujitsu Yourself

You and I are extraordinary creatures. But too often we think of ourselves as just average. What we fail to realize is what remarkable capacities we have.

One reason most organizations settle for low performance is that managers almost universally underestimate both their own capacities and the potential of those who work with them. Most of us tend to *jujitsu* ourselves.

Jujitsu is the art of using someone else's strengths for one's own advantage. We practice a sort of reverse jujitsu when we use our own strengths against ourselves. We tend to overstate the capacities of other animals, such as the navigational ability of migratory birds and the communications skills of dolphins, and stand in awe of machines like computers. At the same time, we do a good job of finding our own flaws. Don't we make silly mistakes in our checkbooks? Aren't we forgetful? Don't we often jump to illogical conclusions? But what we ignore by focusing on our minor defects is the fact that we have extraordinary minds and remarkable abilities.

Our brains make us unlike any other animal on this earth, and our unique capacity to sense and structure the world within our minds and to communicate these ideas to others makes us both different from and superior to any other living creature.

Scientists believe that after the baboons left their mountain homes, it took 100,000 years for their toes to adjust, via evolution, to living on flat land. Modern humankind appeared on earth only 40,000 years ago. In less than 10,000 years our ancestors have filled the earth with houses, roads, hospitals, and factories, and invented languages and created poems and paintings along the way.

In my management workshops I ask participants these questions:

- Can you name 30 birds and 30 flowers in 5 minutes?
- Can you multiply 63,542,742 by 11 and write the answer in one step?
- Can you memorize the order of 20 objects in 10 minutes and know the location of each object two days later?
- Can you think of 20 additional ideas on any subject after you think the well has run dry?

Virtually all the participants answer no to these questions. But after the workshop, everyone answers yes. They can, in fact, do all these things. They either lacked the knowledge, skill, or the right attitude. They jujitsued themselves.

We marvel at ants. Their colonies seem so complicated and totally integrated. Yet an ant has only 500 brain cells. We lose more than this number of neurons by consuming one glass of wine. Our brains have more than 10 billion neurons—as many as there are stars in the sky. If each neuron could only touch two other neurons, the number of possible configurations in our brains would be two to the 10 billionth power, a number that would take 90 years to write out at one second per digit. In reality, each neuron connects with thousands of others, and the possible number of configurations in our brains is too large to understand using any metaphor!

Our brains make up about 3 percent of our body weight, but it takes 30 percent of our blood supply to feed and cool this fantastic organ. The typical brain weighs about 2½ to 3 pounds. There are no moving parts. If you held a brain in your hand, it would feel like a balloon filled with 6 cups of water. Unlike a telephone system, the brain has thousands of different pathways that a message can follow. It's been estimated that a single brain contains sixty times the switching power of the entire U.S. telephone network. The storage capacity of the human brain makes a computer look like a bird's brain. According to Dr. Herbert Simon of Carnegie Mellon University, the mind can hold 100 trillion bits of information. Even if this estimate is wrong by 99 percent, the average mind has several billion times the storage capacity of any computer.

If you're still not convinced of the magnificent power of your mind, consider your retrieval system. There is no machine like it. To see why, try to answer this question: What is Alexander the Great's telephone number?

That's a silly question, right? Yet, even the most sophisticated computer would probably have to search every telephone book in the world before it could respond to that question.

Have you ever smelled fresh bread? Tasted a lemon? Touched a smooth pebble? How can you pull a smell, a taste, a touch—sensations that may be 10 or 20 years old—out of your memory? And although computers can process information faster than humans can, they don't have the capacity to perceive the world or conceive novelty.

The human brain is fantastic, and to say so is neither romantic nor self-congratulatory. We are not machines, and we are not like any other animal.

The question, then, remains why do we use so little of our brains? This is the right starting point for anyone who wants to encourage top performance. Indeed, top managers in consistently high-performing organizations or industries, whether they are coal mines, hospitals, athletic teams, or merchandising firms, share a fundamental idea. They believe that the average person has an immense intellectual and creative capacity and a strong desire to contribute his or her best effort to a significant task. Extraordinary performance is possible with ordinary people because we all have a wealth of unused capacities, waiting to be tapped.

Thinking Like a Magician

All of us have been perplexed by magicians who seem to defy the laws of nature: A woman floats without visible support; a borrowed watch is smashed with a hammer and later found in perfect condition inside a nest of locked boxes; a huge lion materializes inside an empty cabinet. Amazing! Enigmatic!

But why should managers be interested in how magicians—or, more precisely, how the people who invent these magical stunts—think?

Over the last 40 years I've had the opportunity to know several of these magical inventors. At first glance they seem to be almost completely heterogeneous. They differ in educational background, social and political perspective, and mechanical ability; but, they have one thing in common: an unconventional way of thinking. This magical way of thinking can be applied productively to other aspects of everyday life. Here are three principles that these inventive people abide by.

Principle 1: Anything That a Person Can Visualize, Can Be

Most of us live in a world governed by rules and conventions that inhibit us. Since we tend to think along conventional pathways, we are good at finding reasons why we *can't* do something. We visualize impediments with great clarity.

Since all magic is an illusion, creative magicians do not feel limited by what is. In fact, they see no limitations; instead, they mentally visualize how it might look if an elephant were to shrink to the size of a dog, or if the Statue of Liberty should suddenly vanish. Reality becomes an artist's sketchpad, and virtually anything that can be drawn can be actualized.

James Lincoln, the creative force behind Lincoln Electric Corporation in Cleveland, Ohio, set the course for this remarkable manufacturing firm, which has dominated the welding equipment industry for 50 years, by espousing the same philosophy. Lincoln believed that whatever a person could visualize could be. He also believed that cost reductions and product improvements had almost no limitations. And, to date, he has been right. Not only do they have loyal customers, they also have the most productive and highest-paid employees in the industry.

Henry Ford learned a valuable lesson from his former employer, Thomas Edison, who insisted that Ford was limiting his vision with existing technology. (In those days, automobiles were made in carriage shops one at a time.) Ford's engineer told him it was impossible to make an automobile for less than $900. But when Ford visited a cookie factory in Chicago and saw a moving belt bringing materials to stationary workers, he visualized applying the same idea of specialization of labor to a car assembly plant. He tried it, and the price of his cars fell to $500.

If you believe in the impossible, the impossible can be.

Principle 2: There Is More Than One Way of Doing Anything

Not only do these magical inventors believe they can do the impossible, they are also confident that they can find several different ways of attaining the desired result.

Creative bank robbers have this same outlook. Bank vault manufacturers used to advertise their safes as impossible to crack. One such robbery-proof safe was installed in Nice, France. On Monday, July 19, 1976, bank officials discovered that the bank had been robbed of $10 million.

The theft was labeled the heist of the century. Not only did the daring robbers break into the safe, but it was later discovered that they had come up with several ways to do so.

Similarly, astute managers know that there is not just one way to do any thing or to produce any good.

Back in 1961, I was fascinated by the impact of a 30-year-old bank executive in Phoenix, Arizona, who discovered a new way to attract funds to his fledgling bank—by paying depositors daily interest. This was a revolutionary idea since other banks compounded interest quarterly, but it seems so simple in retrospect.

Self-service and prepackaged goods in grocery stores are ideas that are only 60 years old. They seem obvious to us today, don't they?

Like Henry Ford before him, Marcel Bich, founder of the Bic Corporation, came up with an ingenious way to mass-produce a reliable product at a reasonable price when he developed the Bic ballpoint pen in 1949. Prior to his approach, ballpoint pens were costly and often leaked.

Not only do most of us tend to shrink the world by our sense of what can be, we also don't search for alternative ways of doing what we do.

Principle 3: The Simplest Way Is the Most Elegant and Best Way

Inventors of magical effects believe that they can create virtually any feat they desire. Furthermore, they know they can come up with several different ways of accomplishing the desired stunt.

Which method, or *modus operandi,* do they select? Almost always, their choice is the simplest method. They find elegance in accomplishing a lot with a little. For example, in 1920 Harry Houdini was locked naked in a guarded Siberian jail cell. How did he escape? Would you be disappointed to learn that although he knew several ways to free himself, all of which were difficult and risky, he chose to bribe his guard? Such is the stuff of which legends are made.

While a prisoner in a Nazi concentration camp, Jakow Trachtenberg invented a simple but revolutionary way of doing arithmetic, shortening calculation time by 80 percent and improving accuracy. There are no multiplication tables or long division procedures as we know them in his system. Known as the shorthand of mathematics, it uses a series of keys that, once memorized, makes calculations easy, even for those who are poor in math.

The Japanese system of manufacturing, in which parts arrive just in time, simplifies the process. This production approach reduces plant size, inventories, and clutter. The typical Japanese appliance, whether it be a window fan or a camera, will have fewer moving parts than the American equivalent. The German rotary engine is elegant because it, too, uses few moving parts. It has been only a few years since a ticketed airline passenger hasn't had to wait in two lines before boarding a plane. One line is clearly simpler. No line would be even better. There is elegance in simplicity.

What does magical thinking have to do with the more practical things in life? This way of thinking, which apparently is shared by people from all walks of life— from criminals to artists to entrepreneurs—is not a naive or romantic outlook. Quite the contrary. This way of thinking has propelled us upward in all areas of human endeavor.

What we can learn from these magical thinkers is that the impossible is possible, and that the ultimate resource is the human mind.

Taking the Zigzag Approach

We definitely need straight thinkers. In fact, most formal education requires straight thinking, which is used to solve problems of all kinds. For example, if a manufacturer wanted to know how many ski boots she would have to sell to break even, she could use an accounting formula to get a correct answer. If a person wants to know how many gallons of paint to purchase to cover a 20- by 12-foot room, a paint store employee can quickly calculate the right answer. Some straight-thinking problems are complicated, but even the most complicated economics and physics problems use rules, algorithms, and recipes. Every time we do a crossword puzzle, balance a checkbook, bake a cake, or spell a word, we are tapping our straight-thinking skills.

Yet, as important as straight thinking is, it is critical that we learn to blaze new trails with zigzag thinking. Rarely taught to us, zigzag thinking is used to tackle three types of problems.

Type I. Zigzag thinking is used to make small or incremental changes in an existing process or product. Much of the progress in our lives is the result of tens of thousands of zigzag thinkers, each of whom made marginal changes. In most cases, they change what is and add value or reduce cost with their incremental improvements.

When I shower, I pour shampoo out of a plastic bottle into my hand and lather my hair. A plastic bottle is an improvement over a breakable glass one, and the fliptop lid on the screw cap allows me to pour the shampoo without removing the top. Both these innovations are helpful, and there is no doubt that they have improved my life, if ever so slightly.

A patent recently was given to a young man who invented a screwdriver that propels screws into wood without the use of electricity. The force for this operation comes from a motor that is powered by squeezing a handle attached to the screwdriver. This represents a small but potentially significant improvement over the electric screwdriver.

Cost reductions have come about in the transportation industry by the use of new, easy-to-clean tank cars and new types of containers. Self-service in supermarkets and manufacturer-priced merchandise can reduce the cost of marketing. Video cameras replace nighttime security guards, and answering machines replace people who were paid to take telephone messages.

A dynamic world is a changing one, and human beings constantly are finding new and better ways to do things. Zigzag thinking is needed to make these improvements. The optimistic assumption used for Type I zigzag thinking is that there is always a different and better way of doing something. Real-world experience supports this belief. Cooking over an open fire is fine when you're camping, but for everyday use, a gas or electric stove is much more convenient. And a microwave oven is even more time saving.

Since any organization needs to improve constantly, it needs leaders who focus on tomorrow and find better ways of doing what they are doing today. In his best-selling book *A Passion for Excellence,* Tom Peters asserts that there are only two major concerns for a business—customers and innovation. Most outstanding organizations have created an environment that encourages and rewards zigzag thinking. Most of the zigzag ideas will not work. Most oysters do not produce pearls; but to find a pearl, you must be willing to work at it and allow for failure. Possibly the best Type I zigzag thinkers are the Japanese. They didn't invent automobiles, computers, or televisions, but they have added value to the basic products.

Type II. Zigzag thinking is also used for coming up with solutions in which straight thinking does not work. For example, take the case of a driver with a 12-foot, 2-inch rig who's approaching a 12-foot tunnel. The driver could turn around and find an alternate route (straight thinking), or possibly risk trying to barrel his way through (clouded thinking). But instead, the driver lets some air out of his tires, reducing the height of his truck by four inches. Zigzag thinkers invent solutions that seem self-evident and simple after they've been applied.

Many scientific inventions and discoveries are the result of this kind of thinking. The story of Archimedes and the golden crown illustrates this fact. According to the tale, the king of Syracuse, Sicily, had a beautiful crown made of gold. Claiming that he had used four pounds of pure gold, the artisan gave the king a bill for his time and materials. But how could the king be sure that the crownmaker had not mixed the gold with a less expensive metal? The only apparent way to find the answer was to melt down the crown, but this would destroy it. Archimedes's solution, however, was so brilliant that he supposedly got so excited by his zigzag insight that he jumped out of his bath and ran naked through the streets shouting, "Eureka!" ("I've found it!")

His solution was to submerge the gold crown in a vessel filled with water and to capture the displaced water in a container. Next, he submerged a 4-pound bar of pure gold into the same amount of water. The amount of displaced water was the same. If the crown had contained some baser metal, the weight would be the same, but the volume of the crown would be larger because of the presence of a less dense metal. Since sunken objects displace their volume, and the volume was the same in both cases, the goldsmith wasn't fudging.

This is Type II zigzag thinking at its best. Unlike with straight thinking, there is no rule book, recipe, or jigsaw-puzzle box cover to refer to for help. When tackling Type II problems you may go down many roads, come to dead ends, go back, and zigzag about until you find a solution. Type II zigzag thinkers change their focus of vision; they redefine the problem or think sideways.

Type III. If I asked you, "How could you build a better mousetrap?" you could, no doubt, use Type I thinking to suggest all sorts of improvements. When this question was posed by the editors of a science magazine several years ago, the winning solution was quite creative. It called for a mousetrap that looked something like a sweet potato with a flat bottom and a hole at one end. Made of hard plastic, it was hollow. A mouse was enticed into the trap by bait. Once it entered the hole, its body would choke off the air and the mouse would suffocate. The door on the bottom could be opened to dispose of the mouse. The trap had no springs or moving parts. It would never wear out. It worked!

Yet, this mousetrap didn't become a commercial success. Why not? How could the person emptying the mousetrap be sure that the mouse was dead? The only way was to take the bottom off the trap. But what if the mouse was still alive?

The most commonly used mousetrap was patented in the eighteenth century. Why are so many sold each year? Because after the mouse is trapped, the whole trap, including the dead mouse, is tossed in the trash. No one would want to throw away a $12 space-age plastic mousetrap. Although this mousetrap is clever, it is not customer oriented.

A Type III zigzag thinker will approach a problem by redefining it. For example:

> *Person with a problem:* How can I build a better mousetrap?
> *Zigzag thinker:* Why?
> *Person with a problem:* Because I want to catch mice.
> *Zigzag thinker:* Do you really want mice? Why?
> *Person with a problem:* No, I really don't want mice. I want to get rid of mice.

The question now becomes how to get rid of mice or possibly how to keep mice away.

Type III zigzag thinking gives you a whole new definition of the problem. This is the type of thing that Fred Smith, founder of Federal Express, did with his delivery system, and Disney did with EPCOT. A whole new process or approach, a shift in vision and practice, comes from Type III zigzag thinkers. They are revolutionaries.

There is no doubt that we need straight thinking. Accountants, engineers, economists, all of us need high-level analytical skills. But if we are to find better ways to educate children, cheaper ways to provide healthcare, and new ways to reduce crime and pollution, we need zigzag thinkers. And it is not only on a global or national scale that zigzag thinking is needed. Competition among churches, banks, utilities, colleges, hospitals, retail stores, dry cleaners, and wholesalers requires a sustained and passionate commitment to zigzag thinking and its twin sister, innovation. The alternative is to stick to the same old highway, which eventually will deteriorate into a rut.

3

What's Holding Us Back?

You and I are not gods. We are neither omniscient nor immortal. But we are wondrous creatures. Why is it, then, that most of us use so little of our immense capacity? If we use the analogy of an automobile, one might say that we have Porsche brains. But most of us operate like Model Ts. Why? What are the brakes holding us back, and what can be done to release them?

In this chapter, you will be invited to think about the brakes you put on yourself and possibly on those around you. You will find that your wonderful intellect can often trip you up, and that the things you often are most certain about are not true.

Because we bring our previous experiences to new situations, we tend to see things as we believe they are. We also have a tendency to greatly underestimate our capacities and abilities. We say "no" too quickly to all sorts of things that we can do.

Once we understand how frequently we jujitsu ourselves, that is, use our creative and intellectual abilities

39

against ourselves, we can better understand others and know what it takes to be a true leader.

In the essays that follow, you will come across firewalkers, magicians, dwarfs, astronomers, and marketing managers. A strange collection, perhaps, but important lessons can be learned from all kinds of people.

Are You Suffering From Deprivation Dwarfism?

Frederick II, King of the Two Sicilies and Holy Roman Emperor in the thirteenth century, was a brilliant scholar and linguist. In his middle years, he came up with a provocative theory. Frederick believed that each person was born not with a blank slate for a mind, but with inherent skills and abilities. For example, he hypothesized that speaking was a natural, not a learned, ability. Although language varied throughout the world, he believed that everyone was preprogrammed to speak a particular tongue, and that a person would start using that language as soon as he or she was physically able to speak.

Being of a scientific bent, Frederick decided to test this hypothesis. He set up a nursery with separate cubicles and gathered several newborn babies from different cultures. Each child was cared for in total isolation by a surrogate mother who was given strict instructions. She was to feed and bathe the children, but she was never to speak or in any other way interact with them.

Did the babies eventually begin to speak different languages? No, for they all died within the year. Apparently, they could not live without nurturing words and human affiliation.

Is this story apocryphal? A folk tale?

It probably is. But twentieth-century scholars have abundant evidence of the impact of emotional deprivation on the mental and physical health of children. A study of children placed in German orphanages after World War II showed that those in a group that was given ample affection and positive support by the headmistress had better health and growth patterns than a similar group of children that was given the same diet but a harsh and threatening matron.

Lyton Gardner published similar findings in an article entitled "Deprivation Dwarfism" in *Scientific American* in 1972. Gardner studied six short and underweight children and found that their bone structure was years behind their chronological age. The striking thing about his study is that all these children came from hostile family environments. Their physical growth pattern reflected an emotional situation and was not genetically caused. When these young children were placed in a new environment in which they felt secure and were given affection, their physical health improved: They gained weight and started to grow. When the children were sent back to the hostile homes, their growth problems recurred.

Most of us know or can imagine how stressful it is to be in an environment that's void of mutual respect, dignity, trust, concern, and love. In a metaphorical sense, the concept of deprivation dwarfism, therefore, is relevant to managers. Isn't it true that some organizations have men and women with retarded growth patterns—not physically, but in terms of professional and personal development? Isn't there a relationship between the work environment and performance?

Twenty years ago, I was lecturing at a summer institute on economics for grade-school teachers in West Virginia. A stout, middle-aged woman in the workshop had recently been singled out by a presidential commission as one of the outstanding teachers in America. She seemed dowdy and not at all charismatic. I learned that she taught at a school in one of the poorest counties in the state, that her school facilities were antiquated, and she had no budget for supplies. Many of her students came from third-generation welfare families; some of the children slept three or four to a bed.

"How," I asked her, "could you get high performance in what appears to be an impossible situation?"

"Those hill folks want their children to be successful, and we find ways," was her reply.

Imaginative, persistent, and committed, she used Sears catalogs to teach math and reading, outdated wallpaper as murals, and the hills and fields as a nature lab. She motivated fifth-grade students to write about mountain folklore and to found, publish, and deliver the village's only newspaper. Where others might have seen dwarfs, she saw bright and strong persons in the making. Her philosophy and approach were contagious; other teachers in the school followed her lead, and this impoverished community took pride in the attainments of its children.

Let's turn to the other side of the world. Japan's manufacturing superiority is partially attributable to an American, W. Edwards Deming, who found an eager audience for his ideas on quality control in Japan and virtually no interest in the United States.

Now in his nineties, Deming is an outspoken critic of American management. He believes that robots, auto-mation, computers, and other examples of modern capital have little to do with Japan's manufacturing performance, for anyone can buy equipment. Rather, he believes that Japanese success has to do with superior production systems—inventory, plant layout, product flow—and superior use of the work force. Everyone at Toyota, for example, is accountable for quality control and product movement. Many American workers, Deming asserts, suffer from deprivation syndrome because they are not given demanding and interesting tasks and are frequently treated like children.

Thirty years ago, I had an experience that proved to me that Deming is right. The corn refining company I worked for had a small consumer products division in Indiana. This factory bottled a pancake syrup that had garnered a good market share in the Midwest. There was nothing wrong with the product, but production costs were excessive.

The plant employed around forty people, most of them farmers' wives. The plant manager, a former Navy officer, boasted about his tight-ship management style. He was intimidating. "Fear and strict enforcement of my policies and rules is all that's needed when dealing with poorly educated workers," he said to me in front of a group of female employees. "Look," he said as he pointed to the women working on the line, "I am managing mental midgets."

The factory operated fairly well—as long as he was on the plant floor. But when he was out of sight or away from the factory, the workers slacked off, and in one case some of them deliberately sabotaged a bottling machine.

A new manager took over during that summer. He invited all the workers to take home a case of the syrup and to try to come up with ideas on how the package or the product could be improved. He established work groups to examine each step in their particular process area and asked the workers to come up with ways to make the job safer, easier, and, if possible, more efficient. The women in each group selected their own leader, with the new manager's approval.

By Christmas the place was humming. There was no new equipment, but the plant was freshly painted, pictures hung on the walls, and often there were fresh flowers and plates of homemade cookies in the coffee room. The labeling line was reorganized, inventories were reduced, and productivity was on the upswing.

By the following summer, the employees had earned a bonus through cost reductions. Productivity improvement committee meetings were held each week on company time—this was three decades before quality circles became the vogue. But the most remarkable change was the reduction in turnover and absenteeism. Within a year, both were negligible.

Without being romantic or utopian, I think it's clear that an environment at work, home, or school that's nurturing, stimulating, and secure can change mental attitudes and physical behavior. After all, deprivation dwarfism is not just a children's malady.

Lowell's Syndrome

One of the world's highest ranking astronomers at the beginning of the twentieth century was an American named Percival Lowell. From his observatory in Flagstaff, Arizona, he verified a hypothesis put forth by Giovanni Virginio

Schiaparelli, a turn-of-the-century Italian astronomer, who believed that there were canals on the planet Mars. Furthermore, Lowell noted that those canals were red and seemed to move. In his book, *Mars As the Abode of Life*, he not only described his findings, but he also drew intricate maps of the canals. His ideas and maps of Mars appeared in textbooks around the world. I remember seeing them in a sixth-grade text 40 years ago.

In fact, however, there are no canals on Mars. Lowell, the meticulous scholar, was suffering from a rare eye disease. When he looked through the telescope, he saw the red veins of his own eyes. But because he was so preeminent, other astronomers didn't challenge his findings—at least not at first.

Most of us suffer from the same type of problem, even though we don't have this biological disease. We frequently make decisions on the basis of what we think we see rather than on reality. I call this Lowell's Syndrome.

For example, on September 17, 1862, General Ambrose Burnside ordered his Union troops to cross the Potomac River and engage in close battle with their Confederate enemies who were on the run. Burnside's troops marched across the bridge at Antietam two abreast. Meanwhile, the Confederates had established excellent positions for their gunners to focus on this target. The result: a horrible slaughter of Union troops. The irony of this battle was that the Potomac was only some 30 inches deep on that day. The troops could have crossed safely at any spot along the river.

Aunt Jemima Pancake Mix is a perfectly good product. But a visiting professor from Nigeria told me how horrified some people of Nairobi were to see this package in their stores. They knew that the pictures on the outside of containers—peaches, beans, potatoes—indicated what was inside. What in the world, then, was in this box, they wondered. Ground-up women? Meanwhile, other Nigerians were offended by the image on the package, perceiving it as an example of Western racism. Needless to say, the product did not sell in that country.

Some years ago, Pepsodent tried to sell its toothpaste to the people of Southeast Asia. The American jingle, "You'll wonder where the yellow went when you brush your teeth with Pepsodent," didn't go over so well in this part of the world. Some of the people of the area chewed betel nuts, which blackened their teeth. Since these nuts were relatively expensive, blackened teeth were a sign of affluence, not a problem to be controlled with Pepsodent or any other toothpaste.

But it is not just generals and business executives who suffer from Lowell's Syndrome. Most of us see reality according to our own preconceptions.

Two years ago, I was sitting in the Dallas airport waiting for a connecting flight. I was tired and chilled from a day spent lecturing in Iowa. A large and unattractive woman approached the area where I was sitting. She must have been 75 pounds overweight and wore boots, dirty blue jeans, a brown work shirt, and a stained leather vest. She sat next to me and lit a cigarette. I looked at her hands; they were coarse and grease-marked. On her right hand she had tattooed a vulgar four-letter word. I hoped she would not talk to me. But in a friendly and pleasing voice, she asked me where I was going.

"Shreveport," I responded, hoping to prevent any further conversation.

"Shreveport," she said. "I know the town well from

my military days. Do you know Spencer's bike shop there?"

She went on to tell me how much she liked to fix things and how mechanical she was. Then she told me she was going home to Memphis after living for 2 months in a Mexican town I had never heard of.

"What were you doing in Mexico?" I asked.

Upon hearing my question, the woman's demeanor changed. Her voice softened and her violet eyes darkened as she related her story. She and her friends were on a motorcycle trip in Central Mexico when her bike broke down. Needing some parts, she let her friends go on without her. She was invited to stay at a Catholic mission and, being industrious, she set to work fixing things. She told me she could do almost anything—masonry, plumbing, and electrical work, as well as repairing machinery. Although it had been 7 months since her bike had broken down, she chose not to rejoin her friends, but stayed on at the mission.

"I'll bet you're making lots of money with your skills," I said, immediately realizing the stupidity of my remark.

"No, I only get room and board," she answered. "Now I am going home to visit my friends and take my $2,100 of savings and return to Mexico."

"Why in the world are you going to take your life's savings out of the bank and return to this mission in Mexico?"

She looked me in the eye and I sensed that she had a secret or something passionately important in her life. Just then, her flight was called and, as this large woman in work clothes stood up and moved toward her gate, she said, "I am going back to the mission because they need me, and I need them."

How many people in that airport were going where they really were needed? Was I? How could I have been so haughty? So judgmental? What kind of life did this woman have? What would it be like to be so physically unattractive?

Then I thought, had I just met a saint in the making? Who knows?

Moving canals, deep river waters, attractive teeth, and human ugliness can be red veins in our own eyes.

Seeing vs. Believing: The Benefits of Great Expectations

From behind a lectern, Jerry Andrus, a famous inventor of optical illusions, addressed a psychology class at the University of Oregon: "You no doubt believe that I'm standing behind this lectern." He pushed it away and there he was, apparently kneeling on a high stool that was covered with a cloth. He looked out at the surprised audience and said, "Now you believe I am kneeling on a high stool. Watch." He reached behind his body and pulled off two mannequin legs and then pulled the drape away from the sides of the stool. He was actually standing inside the stool!

Is seeing believing or is believing seeing?

Sometimes during my management lectures I do the following stunt, which Andrus invented. I take a card case from my pocket and remove the cards, casually shuffling them. One card is selected and initialed. This card is slowly placed into the deck. Without any conjuring moves, the top card is turned over and it is the same initialed card. Impossible!

The demonstration is done again, but this time very slowly. How can this be? It is repeated a third time with everyone watching carefully.

Then I take the initialed card and set it aside. I announce that the card will now dematerialize and then materialize back on top of the deck. The top card is slowly turned over, and it is the initialed one.

"Now," I say, "I don't think very many people in this audience really believe that when this signed card was placed in the deck it rose on an invisible elevator to the top. Nor do very many of you actually believe that this card somehow dematerialized and reappeared back on the deck. You saw it, but you don't believe it, even though every one of you believes I am holding a deck of cards in my hand."

I then toss what everyone thinks is a deck of cards into the air. But it is not a deck of cards; it is a solid block of plastic. I never had more than three cards in my hand during the whole demonstration, but everyone believed I had a full deck.

We often see what we believe. If we believe people are basically vipers, we will find lots of snakes. On the other hand, if we believe people are capable of achieving great things, they stand a better chance of doing so.

About a decade ago, an experiment that illustrates this fact was conducted in a fifth-grade class in California. At the beginning of the school term, the teacher was told that five of the students had been tested and found to be gifted. In fact, these children were quite average. The teacher changed her perceptions of and expectations for these students, and their performance soared well above average.

Twenty years ago, I had an even more dramatic experience that proves this point. I taught a short course on memory improvement to a dozen prisoners in a maximum security prison. I told them that I had examined all their records (the average I.Q. was around 85) and thought they had huge reservoirs of ability that they never used. I said this to them because it was true for them as it is for most of us. I then told them that I was going to teach them the same material I was teaching to an honors seminar of twelve students, and that I expected them to surpass the performance of my college class. I told them it would be hard, that they needed to practice the exercises I gave them, and that I absolutely believed they could do it.

I taught them a basic mnemonic system for memorizing long lists of items. The system requires making strong visual images. How did they do? Can you imagine an examination in which you're asked to read a 100-page issue of *Time* and then be able to describe in some detail what was on every page a week later?

The results still impress me. The convicts outperformed my honor students by a large margin, and all but two could recall at least ninety-five pages of the issue of *Time* they had studied. In fact, they did better than I did on the same exam. My below-average students were able to outperform their professor.

Do we find flaws and defects in our children, our spouses, and our employees because we see them, or do we find these shortcomings because we believe they are there? Maybe the answer is a little of both.

All of us have a strong tendency to grow into the person that others believe we are. Treat employees as though they are crooks, and you will get that response. Treat employees as though they need to be constantly checked by a supervisor, and you will find quality and productivity sagging. Treat people as though they are interchangeable parts, and you will find no loyalty or special effort. Treat adults as though they are children, and you will get childish behavior.

If we believe that every person has immense creative and intellectual capacity no matter what formal education they have, we will find it. If we believe that people have great dignity and integrity and treat them this way, we will find that this is how they see themselves.

There is absolutely no doubt in my mind that there can be a significant improvement in the performance of any organization—restaurant, factory, bank, church, school, or government agency—if managers are convinced that so-called average people are endowed with mental capacities that they want to use to improve productivity. When Fred Smith of Federal Express says his motto is "People, service, profits," he is making it clear that people (his employees) come first.

People respond according to your expectations. If not challenged, they will maintain the status quo. Treat them according to the capacity they have to become, and you will help them grow into what they aspire to be.

Every high-performing organization that I have studied in the last 20 years has one thing in common: *great expectations*.

One reason why the conductors at the world-renown Interlocken Music Camp in Michigan get outstanding musical performances from young musicians is that they expect each person to give his or her best—they will not accept anything less.

Vince Lombardi treated all the Green Bay Packers alike, like dogs. But few people, if indeed anyone, ever expected more from each person than did Lombardi. And he expected more because he saw the capacity that each player had.

High performance requires hard work and high standards. All of us want to be part of an organization that asks us to give our best for something that's meaningful. Being part of a winning team—whether on a hospital staff, in a work group, or in a church choir—is an energizing, exhilarating experience.

Management starts at the top. What are your expectations for both yourself and those who report to you?

The Intelligence Trap

Our minds are truly amazing. Yet, the very thing that makes us superior in most ways to all other animals and computers—our intelligence—can be the very thing that imprisons our minds and impedes our effectiveness. I call this phenomenon the intelligence trap.

If, for example, someone showed me a different and more effective way to brush my teeth, do long division, or grill a steak, I might give it a try and, if it worked, change my behavior. But let someone try to change my mind about an idea that I have thought deeply about and that person will be in for a tough argument. I will direct all my creative and intellectual capacities to the defense of a concept I believe to be right. My mind will scan my mental warehouse for appropriate counter arguments and for specific cases from history, and I will poke holes in what I am certain is a fallacious argument. This phenomenon—the intelligence trap—seems to be part of the human condition.

Albert Einstein is considered one of the more fluid thinkers of this century. Bertrand Russell, the British philosopher, believed that Einstein's real gift was not in calculating (which he was poor at) or in laboratory research (which he never did), but in his capacity to invent new metaphors. Like a poet, he asked himself, "What would the world look like if I took a ride on a light beam?" That metaphor changed our world view.

Yet, Albert Einstein is reputed to have been, at least once, imprisoned by his own intelligence. As the story goes, young Einstein was on vacation in a small Austrian city when he decided to see a hypnotist perform at the local theater. The hypnotist performed a stunt that supposedly perplexed Einstein the rest of his life.

A woman in the audience was invited to the stage and asked to take a handful of coins from a large glass bowl holding over 200 coins. The performer also took a handful of coins and then both of them turned away and silently counted their coins. Then the hypnotist dramatically announced to the woman that he had the same number of coins in his hand as she had in hers plus three extra coins and enough left over to make the total in her hand the equivalent of $6.

The coins were counted and all three statements were verified. The audience applauded. How could this be?

Einstein quickly figured that the entertainer somehow had a way of determining how many coins were left in the bowl. Possibly, Einstein reasoned, there was a delicate scale under the bowl or the bowl was calibrated in some way that would disclose this information. In any case, the problem seemed banal.

Next, the performer invited the woman to take another handful from the bowl. But this time the mentalist first took out a handful of coins and turned away as the woman reached in for her handful. Then without either of them counting the coins he announced that he had the same number of coins as the woman had in her hand plus six more and enough left over to make the woman's total equal the equivalent of $5.25. The performer's coins were counted as they were dropped back into the bowl and the last coin did make the total $5.25. The audience gasped, so did Einstein.

Einstein was stymied. Many years later he is said to have related this incident to his colleagues at Princeton University, but no one could find the solution.

Einstein had built an intellectual prison from which even he could not escape. While his analysis of the first half of the stunt was a logical solution, it was not what happened in reality. But his mind would not or could not overrule this self-evident starting point. His brilliant mind created a rigid prison.

When I replicate this stunt for intelligent adults they are generally perplexed. Yet when I do the same demonstration for a class of 10-year-old children, two or three immediately see the solution. How can a 10-year-old outthink Einstein?

One evening, I went up to my son David's room. He was about 10 at the time and was busy at work on a personal computer program. I had just completed a workshop for General Electric engineers and researchers in which I presented what seemed like a simple problem. At the end of the workshop those bright men and women were still hotly debating the answer. I wanted to see if a child could do any better.

"David," I said, "I have a problem for you. Assume you have two glasses. One has 10 ounces of water and the other has 10 ounces of wine. You spoon out one ounce of wine and stir it into the water glass. Now you take one ounce of the solution from the water glass and stir it into the wine glass. Is there more wine in the water glass than there is water in the wine glass?"

The answer seemed obvious to me. Since you put a spoon of pure wine in the water glass and a spoon of solution back in the wine glass, there must be more wine in the water glass. Right? Wrong! There is the same amount of water in the wine glass as there is wine in the water glass.

David looked up, thought for about 30 seconds, and then asked me if the glasses had the same amount of liquid in them both at the start and at the conclusion. When I told him they did, he said, "The answer must be the same, and it doesn't make any difference how many times you keep switching spoons of water and wine back and forth. It will always be the same."

I am still impressed with his response. Not only was my 10-year-old able to give me the right answer, but he also was able to explain that the answer would always be the same no matter how many exchanges took place.

Many magicians have a lot of practice at flexible thinking, yet even a world-class authority in this field can fall into the intelligence trap. Following my lecture and demonstration at one of the oldest and most respected magical societies in the world, I was invited by one of Europe's finest magicians to have dinner. Over salmon and wine we talked about subtle psychological principles. Mostly I listened with a sense of awe at the depth and breadth of this man's knowledge. He was truly a master.

As the evening came to an end, he offered to show me a method he was working on to determine the identity of a card taken from a deck. His ingenious solution required running through the remaining fifty-one cards twice, making some rapid calculations, casting out nines, and finger counting. All in all, quite difficult.

I asked him to secretly remove two cards and then give me the deck. I dealt the remaining fifty cards one at a time face up on the table, paused, and then announced the names of the two missing cards. I was correct!

The next morning at 7:30 a.m. I got a phone call. My new friend had had a sleepless night. Had I marked his cards? Had I used a convex mirror? Was there a confederate in the room? What mathematical relationship did I know that he did not?

The solution is probably perfectly obvious to you. I made a mnemonic image of each of the 50 cards and then I sorted them out in my mind by suits until I came to cards that I had not seen. Mine had been a straightforward demonstration of a memory feat.

My friend did not believe the explanation. To this day he believes I used some gimmick or guile. His mind, which is so conditioned to bold and subtle chicanery, has been imprisoned by his own superior intellect.

Almost every stockbroker I have known over 30 years believes he or she can pick winners. They all have theories. Some use complicated charts; others have computer models or rely on their own reaction to announcements in the press or analysis of financial records. When their theory of investment seems to work—and it does, on average, half the time—the broker believes he or she has a good useful model. Sometimes the model produces a series of hits and the broker (or investment promoter) becomes intellectually locked into this view. Yet, does anyone really know which securities will rise or fall?

Economists, and I am one, have been intellectually locked into a view of macroeconomics—how the economy works in aggregate—which seems quite shaky today. They have a logical explanation of employment and inflation. But does it actually apply to the real world?

Freudian psychology is built on a metaphorical way of viewing man's inner self. Some of the images and classifications come from Greek classics, which fascinated Freud throughout his life. Is this an intelligence trap? Is this the best way to understand human behavior?

Like physicists, engineers, stockbrokers, economists, psychologists, and everyone else, managers can fall into the intelligence trap. In the past, managers have argued with honest conviction that time clocks were necessary, that women couldn't do men's work, that salaries were a good idea for managers but not for ordinary workers. They have had great confidence in their theories of advertising, human motivation, and pricing.

One pundit summed up the idea of the intelligence trap with this pithy thought: It isn't what you don't know that hurts you, but what you think you know and don't that does you in.

What is it that you are most confident about in your profession or business? What self-evident and obvious conclusions do you hold about your customers' buying behavior, your employees' capacities, or your competitors' actions or reactions?

If Einstein fell into this trap, what about the rest of us?

Managers, Firewalkers, and Saying "No" Too Quickly

You and I have extraordinary creative capacities. No computer can match us in terms of inventiveness. We do not, however, process information as flawlessly or as rapidly as computers, nor are we programmed to unerringly stay on the same course. We can choose to quit. But sometimes we quit too soon. Often a little more effort will bring victory, but we stop just short of the threshold. And the sad thing is we will never know how close we had come. Why do we do this?

One reason is that we have a tendency to discount our own capacities. We are quick to find our own faults and foibles. We denigrate our own abilities when we make such statements as, "You know I have a terrible memory," or "I never was any good at math," or "I'm not creative," or "That task looks too hard for me."

At the start of my workshops on creative thinking, I ask the participants such questions as:

- Can you name 50 different birds in 3 minutes?

- Can you name 30 different flowers in 2 minutes?

- Can you multiply a 20-digit number by 11 and write the answer in one step?

- Can you tie a knot in a rope without letting go of the ends?

- Can you lift 200 pounds over your head?

- Can you memorize 12 objects in order and recall them perfectly 2 days later?

• Can you take any problem and redefine it 5 different ways?

When I ask each of these questions, I also ask for a show of hands. Few are raised. At the end of the workshop, I ask these same questions, and nearly everyone raises a hand in response to each one. The participants are smiling and confident about their answers. What happened?

When the participants learned a few simple techniques of speed mathematics, they could do rapid calculations. When they learned a mnemonic system, they could easily memorize twelve, fifteen, or even twenty items. When they learned simple, creative thinking techniques, they could generate dozens of ideas almost at will.

Many things are actually easier to do than they seem to be; yet, we often say, "No, I can't do that" without even trying. Take the California firewalking craze. Some corporations were paying $300 a person to send their employees to a confidence-building workshop that culminated with the participants walking over a 15-foot path covered with hot coals. The participants would take off their shoes and socks and, after some psychic cheerleading and meditation, gingerly walk over the coals. After the walk, most of them experienced a high, a joyful exhilaration. They had overcome their fears and did something that few could claim to have done, something they were glad they did, but that they would probably never want to do again. Their emotions were real, but the seminars they attended were full of nonsense.

The participants could have walked across the coals with 5 minutes of instruction. In fact, several science professors in California have had hundreds of students duplicate the stunt. Walking on hot coals has little to do with mental powers—it depends on basic physics principles. If you put your hand in an oven heated to 500° Fahrenheit and quickly pull it out, your hand will not be burned; however, if you touch the wall of the oven, you will be burned. The participants walked quickly, the bottoms of their feet were moist from the surrounding grass, and the coals were covered with ash. Although the temperature of the coals was high, the burning contact was low.

On a much more mundane scale, the same phenomenon occurs when I ask people to name fifty birds. They say they can't do it. Then I ask them to call off names of birds one can eat (chicken, turkey), which I list on a chalkboard. Next I ask for birds that live around water; then big birds, small birds, birds in the zoo, birds in backyards, birds kept in houses. In less than 2 minutes, I might have a list of not fifty but seventy-five birds. My workshop participants knew the names of more than fifty birds all along; they just thought the task was too daunting to attempt.

Years ago I was at a sales convention, and the owner of a large bottling plant happened to sit at my table. "Barrie," he said, "I wondered whatever happened to you. You know you called on me frequently and then you stopped. I had just about decided to place our order for chemicals with your company, but when I didn't see you, I gave it to another company. I understand we're one of their largest caustic soda customers now."

Knowing when to fish and when to cut bait—that takes wisdom. Apparently, I had stopped calling too soon.

Thomas Edison, the man who lit up the world, was only a few days ahead of a French inventor who also developed an incandescent lamp. Edison might have given up. He tried hundreds of different items in his incandescent globe until he put a piece of carbonized bamboo in and sent a current through it. Edison did not talk about his hundreds of failures, but about the hundreds of experiments that taught him what did not work. What all our organizations need is more people who, like Edison, have the willpower, the tenacity, and the confidence to try again and again. Our schools, churches, and businesses need people who refrain from saying "no" too quickly.

The story of *The Little Engine That Could*, who said, "I think I can, I think I can, I know I can, I know I can," is considered a children's classic. But all of us can learn a valuable lesson from it. We cannot do everything just because we want to, but many of us underestimate our abilities. We say "no" too quickly to things we can do or can learn to do. Sometimes all it takes is one more step to find the pathway rising to meet us.

Beware of Mental Anchors

What is a boat anchor? What is its function? You know both answers. You also know that an anchored vessel will remain close to its anchor. Mental anchors perform the same function.

Mental anchors may be good things. Our minds can become focused on a small area and we can work assiduously on a topic or problem without being distracted. However, mental anchors can create problems. There is a strong tendency for not only professional managers but for all human beings to drop anchors. For example, we often come to a conclusion about a person or a situation and, no matter how overwhelming the contrary evidence may be, we hold fast to our original conclusion.

Everyone has heard the story of the sinking of the *Titanic* on her maiden voyage in April 1912. Few persons know what a really tragic event this was, and that it could have been avoided. Even after the ship's collision with the iceberg, an additional two-thirds of the passengers who died could have been rescued if it hadn't been for false beliefs.

The *Titanic* was designed to be unsinkable. The steel ship had a double bottom and sixteen watertight compartments. It was widely believed to be the safest boat ever constructed, and this belief was shared by designers, engineers, officers, crew members, owners, and passengers, as well as by the public at large. This belief in the unsinkability of the *Titanic* led to the ship's tragic end.

The *Titanic* set out from England to establish a new speed record. Its destination was New York City. Normally, ocean-going ships carry a sufficient number of lifeboats to accommodate everyone on board. Not the *Titanic*. It carried only enough lifeboats for one-third of the passengers. Furthermore, no practice drills were held for the evacuation of the *Titanic*.

The ship's log first recorded a warning of icebergs in the steamer lane three days out on the ship's voyage. The message was ignored. A second warning was sent, but the radio operator didn't even respond. The *Titanic*—the mighty *Titanic*—was, after all, unsinkable.

Another warning came a few hours later, but neither the captain nor the manager of the White Star Line, who also was aboard the ship, was concerned. The *Titanic* plowed ahead at 22 knots per hour.

By 9:30 p.m., the *Titanic* recorded five warnings of icebergs, with the last report noting that the ship was on a collision course. The only precaution taken was to instruct the night lookout to stay alert.

Two hours later, at 11:32 p.m., the following message was radioed to the *Titanic* by a sailor on the *Californian*, a ship that had gotten stuck in an ice jam: "Say, old man, we are stuck here, surrounded by ice."

The *Titanic*'s operator replied, "Shut up, shut up, keep out. I am talking to Cape Race; you are jamming my signal." The unsinkable pride of the White Star Line steamed on.

At 11:40 p.m., a giant iceberg was spotted straight ahead—but it was too late. The *Titanic* smashed into an immovable mountain of ice, and its steel bottom received a gash as long as a football field. The supposedly watertight doors and bulkheads gave way and the unsinkable *Titanic* bowed down and began to sink.

Many of the passengers did not believe the ship could really be in danger. Lifeboats were thrown into the water but, because no drills had been conducted, they carried away at least 500 fewer passengers than they could have.

Distress signals were sent from the *Titanic* within minutes of the collision. The *Californian* was only a few miles away, but the radio operator had gone to bed after having been told to shut up. Other crew members aboard the *Californian* saw the *Titanic*'s rocket signals, but they did nothing except to try to communicate by blinker. Ironically, the *Californian* could have pushed through the ice field and helped rescue the *Titanic*'s passengers, for the night was clear and the sea was calm.

It took the unsinkable *Titanic* less than three hours to sink. Help arrived too late for the 1,513 people who perished as a result of the collision.

Mental anchors are easy to see in dramatic incidents like the sinking of the *Titanic,* but other examples are all around us. Just think about these questions:

- Why are banks called commercial banks? How would a bank operate if someone like Sam Walton ran it?

- Why is it that consumer traffic on railroads has declined? What would happen if the Walt Disney Company took over a major railroad?

- Why is it that we spend more on healthcare per capita than any other country in the world and, in many ways, we are less healthy than citizens of other developed countries?

Managers in different industries get anchored to a certain perception of reality and sometimes, in spite of the evidence, they persist in holding on to their mindset. For example, bankers may talk about consumer orientation, but they often are anchored to a different position; despite evidence that a growing number of parents are placing their children in private schools, public school administrators hold tightly to their old anchors; medical practitioners continue to stress fixing people at almost any cost over preventing problems; many mainline churches react to declining membership either by trying to be all things to all people or holding on to rigid views and policies; and city and Chamber of Commerce leaders often cling to the same ways of promoting and developing communities, even though they yield modest results.

But important decision-makers aren't the only ones guilty of anchoring. You and I may have mental anchors that keep us stuck in the danger zone. Furthermore, we often unwittingly strap others to our anchors. How often has someone (perhaps even you) called a meeting and said something like, "You know why I've called you together." (At this point the others nod their heads even if they haven't the fainest idea as to why the meeting was called.) "I've been thinking about the declining sales in the Memphis market and I think we ought to do what we did in Indianapolis when this happened—double the number of TV ads and offer deep discounts to the dealers. What do you think?"

Here we have a not unusual case of a leader dropping anchor on his particular perception of a problem and proposing a solution without any skeptical analysis. So long as the group stays anchored to the implicit definition of the problem—sales down (which is a symptom and not the cause)—the group is stuck, limited by its own focus. Full steam ahead!

What can we do about these mental anchors? Here are some ideas that might prove helpful:

1. *Examine your organization with a naive questioning approach and invite others to do the same.* Make a list of questions that a person from an entirely different industry might ask.

- Why do people come to your store or office? How do you know your answer is right?
- Why do you want to grow?
- Could your organization be better if it were smaller? Are you sure about your logic?

- What would be going on in your organization if it were run by Toyota or by Sam Walton? Why don't you do these things?
- Why are you organized the way you are? How else might you organize to get things done?
- Why do you spend so much time doing things that others could do while you put off the things that only you can do that will make a difference?

These questions are merely illustrations. What you want is a list of naive yet radical questions that get right to the root of your situation.

2. *Encourage and reward "whys" guys and become one yourself.* Ready, fire, aim as a management philosophy may make some sense in a war zone, but it is not on balance a good philosophy to follow. Every committee from the top to the operative level on the shop floor needs at least one "whys" guy to be skeptical and make the rest of us slow down our decision-making process.

A college board of trustees recently was considering building new parking lots when a "whys" guy (a woman, in this case) asked, "Why do we need more space?" The answer was, for cars, of course. "But why do we have so many cars?" the "whys" guy persisted. The net result was a reduction of cars by requiring a steep car registration fee. The "whys" question slows down the decision-making process so that the right decision, not just any decision, is made.

A person can be selected in each meeting to be an assertive "whys" guy. Civil but dogged, this person will be responsible for challenging assumptions, asking for evidence, and questioning conclusions. This person may be considered a nuisance and will definitely slow down the process. Yet, that is exactly what is needed.

Ready, aim, aim, aim, fire as an approach might have helped some of the ailing firms that recently have fallen victim to a sluggish economy. But their top management, no doubt, didn't see the icebergs as they sped ahead.

We need men and women on deck who will force the rest of us to challenge the ideas we assume to be true. What anchors do you have in your organization? Are you sure you are unsinkable?

Working Like a Beaver

We've all heard the expression "busy as a beaver." Doesn't it conjure up a picture in your mind of an industrious, clever critter? Can't you just see him working away—cutting down trees with his teeth, gnawing them into proper size lengths, and then assembling these logs in a truly amazing fashion? Where does he get his architectural plans? How does he know how to construct these intricate dams?

A few years back I saw a TV special about a team of naturalists studying North American beavers. The scientists wanted to find out how much of a beaver's behavior is learned and how much is instinctive. As you know, beavers build dams in rivers to form a small lake. Along the bank of this lake, beavers dig a tunnel that leads to a cave that they also fashion. The cave is filled with food that the beavers consume during the winter.

Now we have a puzzle. The beaver's small lake freezes over in the winter. How can the beavers get out of this cave if the only exit is through a tunnel whose opening is 3 or 4 feet below the frozen surface? The answer to this enigma is that the river is still flowing and that there is one spot where the river's currents keep the ice that covers the lake from freezing over—or, if it does freeze, it will be thin enough to go through. Beavers somehow know where this hole will be and engineer the dam and the cave entrance in just the right position. Amazing!

The scientists photographed the construction of the dam. They also filmed an unforgettable sight. Something went awry. For some reason—maybe the beaver's mental compass was defective or maybe the river's current changed—when the beaver being studied swam out of the underwater tunnel, he did not go to the hole. Instead, he banged up against thick ice. Bang! Bang! Bang! The camera crew was surprised. They were prepared to film the beaver's exit through an opening that was less than 3 feet away from where the beaver was repeatedly hitting its head against an icy ceiling. Bang! Bang! Bang! Crew members went out on the ice and tried to entice the beaver to swim to the opening. They left food on the ice next to the hole; they tried to attract the beaver with shiny spinners and by calling. No luck.

The beaver would not change its pattern of behavior. It returned to its cave. The following day the same thing happened. Even though the film crew was used to life and death in nature, they seemed anxious and distraught. They wanted to help the beaver, but nothing they did worked.

In the spring, when they dug up the cave along the

bank of the river, the team found four carcasses—two baby beavers and their parents. All four had starved to death.

How could this be? After all, beavers are master builders and assiduous laborers. Why couldn't the beaver move over 3 feet? Three lousy feet! Thirty-six inches is all that it would have taken to preserve this family.

The beaver's brain is hard-wired. Programmed to do the complicated tasks it does, the beaver's brain apparently can't adjust to unexpected events. The beaver stays on track doing the same thing over and over because that is what beavers do. Are you working like a beaver?

I often do. For example, I can recall a particularly busy day when I felt like Mr. Fixit. Several people had called me on the phone or come to see me with problems and I had gotten them all straightened out by the end of the day. I had to work through lunch hour and keep a hard pace of activities—notes, calls, conversations—to do it, but I did, and I felt good about myself.

But do you know what? I did not accomplish a single thing that day. I did not move closer to any significant goal. Nor did I motivate or encourage anyone else to move forward. What did I do all day? I untied knots— knots that I had tied in the first place.

At 8:05 a.m. one of my graduate students called, upset that he had received an F in economics. He told me that he had gotten a B+ at mid-term and that he had written a solid paper and felt good about the final. Would I check into this? Of course I would.

What does checking mean? First, a call to the registrar's office. They had to find the grade sheets and get back to me. Yes, a grade of F had been recorded. Then I discovered that I had made the recording mistake. I had given the F to the wrong person. Now I needed to fill out two forms—one for the student who had gotten the F, stating that it should have been a B, and one for the student who got a B, stating that it should have been an F. Next, I called back the unhappy student and told him of my error; then I had to call the other student. I sent both students a handwritten note apologizing for the confusion. After that, I had to send the correct information to the business office because they had sent out bills to the students' employers. These employers paid a sliding fraction of tuition depending on the student's grade. This error had serious financial consequences. Finally, I had to give the proper information to the departmental assistant who records grades in student folders and on our computer. I untied a complicated knot.

Other similar events happened throughout the day. All of them involved problems or knots. All of them required reworking a defective product or service. All of the time- and energy-consuming things I did were meant to reduce hassle. The business office had been hassled because my office had not communicated the relevant information clearly, and a student had been hassled because of a recording error.

You see, I was working like a beaver. I worked hard at fixing things. I was focused and dedicated to the tasks before me. But if I repeated this type of working day after day, it would be like butting my head against a ceiling. I would make no progress.

There are three types of work: routine work, problem-solving work, and innovative work.

The goal for routine work should be zero-defect. A defect is a hassle. Anytime a person, a coworker, customer, supplier, or you, is hassled, something is out of harmony. Waiting in line to check into a hotel is a hassle. Finding your airplane seat occupied is a hassle. No lettuce in the supermarket is a hassle. A complicated assembly procedure for a child's toy is a hassle. Filling out long forms in a hospital is a hassle. A rude waiter is a hassle. A wrong part is a hassle. Returning your auto to the dealer the day after its maintenance check-up is a hassle. If routine work is done perfectly at every step, there will be little or no hassle. The finished product or service will be delivered in perfect working order; it will be reliable and dependable and it will be there on time. You will not have to ask for a glass of water at a restaurant or look for a clerk to help you in a store. You will not have to call to have grades changed or to receive promotional material.

What we need to do is focus on the routine, the ordinary. How can ordinary things be done in an extraordinary way? McDonald's at its best—even for those who don't like fast food—is a model of doing the ordinary brilliantly. Imagine if McDonald's worked the way I sometimes do. Cheeseburgers ordered, but Chicken McNuggets delivered, and then only after a long wait.

Toyota, Herman Miller, Harley Davidson, Disney, and Wal-Mart try to do things right the first time. In fact, these companies border on being fanatical about this. They want the best people and materials, the best work environment, and the best systems. Each and every step meshes. Rather than fixing products or trying to make people happy after the fact, these organizations aim to eliminate all reworking. Reworking—untying knots—reflects a dysfunctional system, a system that must be fixed.

What does all this mean? Let's go back to my days as Mr. Fixit. All the errors that I made required reworking of the product or situation—and, therefore, added no value. These activities were problem-fixing activities. In fact, all the problems I fixed still left the people less well off than they would have been if there had been no defects in the first place. All the people who called me wasted their time and energy because of defects, and so did I. What needs to be done is to find the cause of our snags, knots, and glitches, and then identify ways to eliminate them. *This is called innovative work—fix the process, not the product.*

One of the most impressive things about a well-run factory or office is how smoothly things run—you can sense it immediately. The place seems to hum. Have you ever had a humming day?

All of us can get stuck in habitual patterns of behavior and find it hard to stand back and see that we are banging our heads without adding any value for our customers. We need to move sideways and find a better path. Beavers can't do this. But we can.

Are you working like a beaver?

4

The +10 Percent Team

Tom Jones Monick, a 31-year-old sales engineer, has no special, natural athletic ability. But through hard work and discipline, he has become an outstanding triathlete. Recently, I told him about a provocative article I had read in a triathlete magazine.

Three men decided to challenge traditional ideas about athletic training. They believed that many athletes train too long and in the wrong fashion. Each of them had a different technical expertise, and they concluded that, working as a team, they could get extraordinary performance from an ordinary athlete using their innovative approach.

They chose a man in his early thirties who had competed in triathlons for years, but with average results. Most high-performing triathletes train full-time, but the novel training program that the three men designed allowed their subject to keep his job. It did, however, concentrate on the areas in which he had the greatest probability of improving.

The candidate's swimming time was poor—around 40 minutes for a mile. The three coaches improved his stroke and breathing and emphasized sprint training. They used a technology that gave him frequent feedback so he knew what his pace was at all times. Eventually, they got his time down to under 25 minutes.

They also reduced the amount of time he spent running and cycling. However, they improved his style and again found ways to give him frequent feedback. Finally, they wouldn't let him push himself to capacity during trials. The goal was to peak during the big race. The result: He came in fifteenth in an open competition with hundreds of outstanding triathletes.

"This is remarkable," I said to Tom, "and isn't it a great metaphor for the power of teamwork? This was a team victory—everyone was needed for this accomplishment."

Tom looked at me with cold eyes. "I don't see the relationship, Barrie. I have never had a boss who wanted to be a coach. They all wanted to be the star, clutching the cup in the winner's circle."

Tom was serious about what he said. He was telling the truth as he saw it.

While there's a time for individual pursuits—writing a poem or flying a kite—most activities involve group cooperation. Large groups—a state university, for example—will be broken into smaller groups, which in turn may be formed into still smaller groups or teams. Most of us are part of relatively small work groups.

Managers at the top frequently implore everyone to pitch in for the common good. But these pep sessions usually have little effect and often demotivate the team.

Many people are surprised to learn that Japanese grade schools are organized around small teams of students. These teams are given challenging assignments and are expected to get everyone to perform at a high level. The youngsters on the teams coach, cajole, and encourage one another. The team's score is their grade. Is this a leveling process? If so, the Japanese have leveled off at the highest level in the world.

This chapter presents some practical ideas on how the team—the work group—can be organized and led in such a way that everyone feels like a winner, a star. Teamwork involves the feelings, attitudes, values, visions, and aspirations of the individuals involved. It requires mutual trust and long-term commitment. The stories and examples that follow are not meant to provide a pat formula for leaders but to show how teams can multiply the strengths of their individual members.

You will read about redwood trees, the Salisbury Cathedral, digital clocks, and Easter Island idols, and you'll even find there's a lesson to be learned from the center of an apple. How can these diverse objects be related to high-performing teams? Read on and find out.

The Metaphor of the Trees

What do trees have to do with leadership and effective teamwork? Plenty—if you look closely enough.

Have you ever see the *Sequoia sempervirens*—the giant redwoods? The height, girth, and dignity of these trees are awe-inspiring. To me, these trees, which grow only in the humid coastal areas of Northern California and Southern Oregon, seem to be supernatural entities—similar to the mythical Greek gods on Mount Olympus. And like the Greek gods, these trees seem to be not only bigger than life, but also immortal.

If you stand next to one of these redwood trees, you will have a hard time seeing it. You have to back away. Imagine a regal redwood with a diameter of 33 feet. It might take twenty-five adults holding hands to ring this tree. The dark brown bark is 10 inches thick. Your eyes lift and you admire the ruler-straight trunk, which is smooth and branchless for nearly 100 feet. Then, long, narrow, drooping branches appear and you notice that they're layered in ascending order with smaller and smaller branches bearing tiny bright green leaves and brown cones. Your eyes finally find the top. This tree is 350 feet tall—as high as a 30-story building. (If it were cut down, it would stretch from goal post to goal post on a football field.) How majestic!

Born of a seed the size of a pinhead, these trees can live for over 2,000 years. The tree we are imagining was a baby when the Roman Empire fell. It was an adolescent when the Arabs invented the zero, a mature adult when Columbus came to America, and a senior citizen when George Washington became our first president. Most fascinating of all is the fact that the coastal redwoods have no taproot.

Do you recall seeing illustrations of an oak or elm tree in your high-school biology textbook? Remember how the major taproot grew deep into the ground—supposedly as deep as the tree was high? Can you picture the whole complicated underground root system, which mirrored the above-ground limb structure and held the slow-growing trees up and gave them nourishment?

But the redwoods do not have this type of root system. Their roots are close to the surface like a palm tree's—and we know that palm trees often are knocked over in a wind storm. How do the redwoods—the world's largest and oldest living plants—stay upright without a deep root system?

The answer is they do not stand alone. They can survive only in a community. Their roots spread out and intertwine with the roots of their neighbors. Their community—called a stand—is interdependent. That is why environmentalists get so upset when someone proposes removing "only a few trees here and there." When "a few" trees are cut down, many perish.

Before we examine how the redwoods can serve as a metaphor for your team and your organization, let's look at another type of tree.

One August, I and twenty-four other college administrators from across the country traveled to Aspen, Colorado, for an education seminar. One afternoon, our leader took us on a picnic and asked each of us to find a quiet spot to reflect on our morning discussion.

I was stretched out on a flat rock near a waterfall. I thought I was dozing. Suddenly, I became irritated by what I took to be whispering all around me. "Why can't some people enjoy the mountains without chattering?" I thought. "Why do they have to be so rude?" I opened my eyes and looked about. No one was there. Then I realized that the sounds I'd heard had been made by the rustling of the leaves of the surrounding quaking aspens.

If the redwoods are mythic gods, these trees certainly are of human proportions. It seemed to me that I could encircle any of these slender trees with my two hands, or for sure with one arm. They are about 40 or 50 feet tall, with a smooth, cream-colored bark. Starting at about 20 feet, narrow branches grow out vertically from the trunk. And from those branches spring 3-inch heart-shaped leaves that are shiny dark green on top and silvery underneath. Long stems support the leaves, allowing them to flutter in the slighest breeze. I think the quaking aspens are the most romantic trees I've ever seen.

When my eye reached the dome-like crowns of the trees, I realized that all the aspens were the exact same height. How could this be?

Sometime later, a forest ranger told me, "These trees grow in high altitudes in North America and they grow where other trees cannot survive. They, like the redwoods, are not found living alone, but always in groves. They huddle together and protect one another."

"But why," I asked, "are they the same height?"

"Because," the ranger said, "if a tree were to lift its head above the others, a blast of wind would come by and cut its top off. There is no room for headstrong superstars in the Rockies."

Anyone who has tried to pull a 1-foot quaking aspen sapling out of the ground knows that it cannot be done. How can this little tree be so tenacious? Does it have a big taproot? No, it doesn't. In fact, the tree's root system is quite shallow—only a few inches below ground. Most saplings are actually root suckers, and all the aspens in a grove are identical, or clones; each and every one is attached to the same mother root. When an aspen dies, it is replaced by a new sprout from the same root system, which is surprisingly large. Some of these systems spread out 100 acres. This means that all the aspens I could see around me from that flat rock above the waterfall were "brothers and sisters."

Now, what lessons can we learn from the redwoods and the quaking aspens? I think they teach us that if an institution—be it a small family or a multinational corporation—wants to survive and flourish over the long haul, it must draw its strength from the voluntary commitment of all its members to give their best effort. Long-term survival and growth, especially in a hostile environment, requires leaders—be they parents or CEO's—who can multiply the strength of individuals by eliciting everyone's cooperation.

Does this mean we cannot be independent, that we cannot stick our necks out, that we ought to conform at all times to the demands of the group? Or does it mean we need team victories? How can you have both the advantage of community and yet provide for independence? What do *you* think the metaphor of the trees has to do with leadership and effective teamwork?

Invisible Foundations

Management seems to have as many fads as the fashion industry. "Corporate culture development" is one idea currently being pitched by both writers and consultants. In fact, there are management consultants who say they can help a firm develop a corporate culture that will make one's employees not only happier, but also more innovative and productive. I'm skeptical of this claim, even though I believe that the proper corporate culture is a crucial ingredient for long-term success. Let me take you on an imaginary trip that will explain why I feel the way I do.

Assume you are walking east on Market Street in Salisbury, England, when you catch your first glimpse of Salisbury Cathedral. Your eye will first see a steeple and then a gigantic stone tower that's 404 feet high. As you walk on, the whole structure, situated in an open field, will come into view. And what an edifice it is! Gothic arches please the eye and the total sight is awe inspiring—precisely what it was meant to be. The cathedral is equally impressive from within. There is a sense of height, breadth, and even puzzlement. How did this glorious and immense structure come into being 800 years ago? The answer makes this church even more remarkable.

Although the cathedral's architect is unknown, the master mason's name is recorded and we know the names of many of the workmen who labored from sunrise to sunset for a penny a day and a bucket of beer. The building stones were rubbed together to make a near perfect fit before they were assembled so that their own pressure—and not mortar—holds them together. The weight of the structure is so great that the solid stone columns have actually bowed out. How can stones bend? The greatest weight is under the tower, which is, in turn, supported by four 6-foot square stones. The project was completed in about 60 years with the simplest hand tools and a wooden winch. One of the first pendulum clocks in England is in the cathedral, and it is still operating, as are the door and window hinges.

To me the really provocative question is not how the workers constructed the cathedral, but how it has managed to stand for so many years. Even with modern technology, it would still be a superb feat to construct a structure that supports 64,000 *tons*. What is even more astounding is that the cathedral is standing in what was once a marshland, with three rivers—two above ground and one underground—flowing only a few hundred feet away.

Experts believe that if this foundation were only 50 feet north or south from its position, the project could not have been completed. How the builders found the proper base rock for the foundation is still a mystery. Some say it was dumb luck; others attribute it to Divine Providence.

Glorious arches, stalwart columns, and heavenly spires do not support themselves. They need firm foundations, even if they are invisible. And as it is for buildings, so it is for all human organizations.

In *The Book of Abraham*, Marek Halter tells the story of the Jewish people. He starts his tale in A.D. 70, when his mythical forebear, Abraham, a scribe, is forced by the Romans to leave Jerusalem. He goes to Alexandria and starts a scroll, which is passed on in the family as it moves to such places as Hippo, Cordua, Narbane, Alsace, Venice, Rome, Constantinople, Amsterdam, London, Canada, and South America.

The saga takes 2,000 years and 800 generations. It is a story of a minority people who suffer, struggle, and survive under what, in retrospect, would seem to be impossible conditions of brutality, persecution, and torment. Why didn't they perish? Why didn't they all give in and convert? It would have been so much easier for them.

How could these Jewish families, time and time again, arrive penniless in a new culture, face new laws, social customs, languages, and traditions, and not just survive but survive with dignity? This appears to be an even more stunning achievement than Salisbury Cathedral. Yet, the magnificent survival in both cases rests on an invisible foundation.

As Halter tells his story, the reader learns over and over that these people, regardless of where they were, believed—no, they *knew*—that the God of Abraham specifically chose them to receive The Law, or the Talmud. The language and rulers of their land could change, but not The Law. It was eternal. These believers knew they were interdependent. They knew they needed one another, and their endurance and strength to survive came from knowing that there would always be someone—a cousin, a distant uncle—who would gladly take them in and help them. This is how it had to be, and this is how it was.

Culture is not something that management consultants can deliver. It does not rest on such organizational trappings as quality circles, profit-sharing schemes, or suggestion boxes. No, culture is the sum total of shared values, attitudes, and beliefs—all of which are invisible and require time to develop.

One of the most fascinating companies in the United States—and possibly in the world—is Herman Miller Corporation. I knew the top managers—sons of the founder—20 years ago when it was a small family-owned business based in Zeeland, Michigan, a town of about 5,000 people.

Even then, the company had a rich heritage. Stories about how well D.J. Depree, the founder, treated his employees during the Depression are still told. From its early years, it was a people-oriented firm, committed to integrity in all relationships. This meant that customers, employees, suppliers, local residents, and even competitors were all treated with great dignity and absolute honesty. Words like fair, just, right, honorable, and compassionate have always been part of the company's vocabulary.

Do nice guys finish last? Sometimes, but not always. Led by Depree's sons Hugh and Max, Herman Miller Corporation has continued to build on the father's cornerstone. A cardinal sin at this company would be to behave in a way that was not "the Herman Miller way." What is this? A universal acceptance of the importance of human dignity and the unequivocal importance of integrity—at all costs.

What was once a small family firm in Zeeland, Michigan, now has over 6,000 employees, ten plants, international customers, and a reputation for quality and integrity. Herman Miller is on the list of *Fortune 500* companies. It is also profitable and one of the most admired business corporations in America.

The breathtaking splendor of Salisbury Cathedral, the magnificent achievement of the wandering Jewish people, and the phenomenal growth of Herman Miller Corporation have one thing in common. All three have invisible foundations that are correctly situated and deep.

When was the last time you checked the foundations of your organization?

How Did They Lift the Stones?

The Sears Tower in Chicago is a strikingly impressive structure. This man-made edifice towers so high that when one looks down from the viewing gallery at the top, the surrounding office buildings look like toys. This Gulliver-like building is highly functional and ugly.

Stonehenge, a prehistoric open-air temple, takes up less space than all the men's rooms on any one floor of the Sears Tower. Yet this circle of stone columns and lintels has captivated men and women for over 3,000 years.

Why is this? Is it because we wonder how a people who had no wheels or pulleys could lift these mammoth stones? Or is it because these ruins somehow link us to some mythic, universal, pristine human need to reach for the heavens? Is there something mysterious about the way the rising sun shoots its rays straight through the diameter of Stonehenge?

Let's be practical for a minute. How did the ancients lift the stones of Stonehenge? All sorts of solutions have been suggested. At one time, some scholars believed the stones were never lifted. Their theory was that holes were dug for the columns and the lintel stones were dragged on top of the buried columns, and then the dirt was excavated. Ingenious, but not right.

Thousands of miles away from Stonehenge, England, another culture living on a small island in the Pacific erected an equally impressive series of monuments. When the Dutch explorers came upon this island in 1772, it was Easter Sunday, and this is how it got its European name—Easter Island. The explorers were mystified by a circle of 6-foot stone pedestals that they found. On top of these stones stood 30-foot stone columns. Faces and torsos were chiseled on each of these stones and all their long faces looked toward the sea. On top of these 40-ton stone faces there were 5-ton stone headpieces. How did those people first lift the stones?

This question puzzled engineers and anthropologists for nearly 200 years. Some hypothesized that the stones were put on rafts and the island flooded. Others thought that the island people fashioned huge balloons to lift the stones. Still others argued that the stones were raised by some arcane power of levitation. Another wild idea was that aliens from another planet had helped erect the stones.

Thor Heyerdahl, a Norwegian anthropologist and explorer, made a special trip to the island with the intention of unlocking the mystery. What did he do? He did something that no physicist, engineer, anthropologist, or any other truth seeker had ever done. Heyerdahl's approach was radical: He asked the local residents!

The method that was used for lifting the stones was part of the oral history of the island, which all the residents learned as children.

How did the natives of Easter Island lift these large stones? Probably the same way the builders of Stonehenge lifted their columns: a little at a time. A crew of men pushed three long, strong poles under one of the block faces. They pushed down and could barely budge the stone, but they could move it a little. They then placed small stones under one end and levered the other. They built a stone bed with larger and larger stones. They raised the stone head above the pedestal, then removed stones from its bed, making an incline. Next, they slid the huge head slowly and tilted it upright on a block where it still stands. No hot-air ballons, levitations, or arcane technology—just a lever and an inclined plane and many hours of hard teamwork were behind this amazing accomplishment. The "secret" was never a secret. The islanders had known the answer all along, but no one before Heyerdahl had ever thought to ask them.

What does this mean for managers of retail stores, banks, hospitals, schools, churches, welfare agencies, and factories? The simple but powerful lesson is that there are ways to lever—to elevate the performance of almost every organization—by implementing Heyerdahl's radical principle: Just ask.

Recently, I told this story to a group of forty-three leaders who were at a management retreat center in Amarillo, Texas. For some reason, when I got to the explanation of the Easter Island puzzle, and I said, "Heyerdahl asked," the audience laughed. Standing in the back of the room was Michael, a bus driver who, though not invited to the conference, was so intrigued by the workshop that he stayed to listen. Angered by the laughter of the participants, he blurted out in a strong voice, "Don't laugh. I know of lots of ways to improve the service and save money for the bus company I work for, but in 17 years no one has ever asked me."

Does asking really work? Consider these cases:

- A factory worker in a Ford auto factory in England saved the company thousands of dollars with a simple, practical alternative to standard operating procedures. Formerly, during the production process, each engine block would come to a work station where a large machine would secure the engine and turn it over. A worker would inspect the borings and cylinders to be sure they were properly oiled and then the block would be turned back over and sent on. The expensive capital equipment used in this process is no longer necessary. The worker now uses a large mirror, similar to the one dentists use, to visually inspect the block. If lubrication is needed, the operator squirts it in with a long-nosed oilcan.

- A night porter in the Hayworth Furniture factory saw fuel where others saw waste. When his supervisor asked for suggestions, he came up with the idea of burning the scrap materials rather than paying to have them hauled away.

- A work team at Donnelly Mirrors Corporation came up with a way of reducing the cost of assembly. Rather than sending wiping cloths to an industrial laundry, the work team bought a washer and dryer, and they wash these cloths during their downtime.

- A secretary in St. Louis sat in on a meeting in which executives were talking about installing a new elevator system in one of the buildings they managed. Tenants in the building were complaining about the long waiting time for elevators. Her suggestion: Install long mirrors next to the elevators. They did and the complaints stopped.

- A truck driver at Prince Corporation thought long-term employees needed special recognition. He remembered the letter sweater he wore in high school and how much it meant to him. Why not establish a program whereby employees could earn points for performance and good attendance? Nothing fancy, but something meaningful. His idea of earning a special jacket and then special badges motivated almost everyone in the factory.

The city below does look different from the executive suites near the top of the Sears Tower. The people look like ants, and there is a sense of power and exaltation that comes from being king of the hill. Others of us sit on smaller mounds, but we still feel powerful. Too bad it's a delusion.

Factory workers, bus drivers, nurses, school teachers, journalists, postal workers, and secretaries are not ants. Customers, clients, patients, and students are not ants. All of us quite ordinary people have extraordinary creative and intellectual capacities. We have knowledge and ideas that can boost the performance of any organization. Ordinary managers must learn what extraordinary managers know—that you and I yearn to be part of an organization that does something worthy and well. We know we can't clean and jerk 50,000 pounds over our heads, but we, as a team, can lever little by little a nearly immovable mass.

If you need some help, just ask.

Everyone an Innovator

All organizations are formed because they can do things with two or more persons that individuals working alone cannot do. Yet, as organizations grow they tend to grow wasteful—not only of materials and money but, probably more important, wasteful of the talents of their members. Most nurses, clerks, production workers, schoolteachers, secretaries, and supervisors believe they can contribute much more than they do.

On the other hand, I know many managers who work hard and love their jobs. They feel stretched by the challenge of their jobs. They are thinking all the time about how they can improve products and processes—reduce hassles, eliminate defects, speed up turnaround time, simplify procedures, and encourage other employees.

Maybe all employees, not just top managers, should own some of the organization's problems. Maybe all employees should share some of the fun—often immense joy—that comes from identifying a problem, finding a workable solution, and then seeing their solution put into action. This is called innovation—the discovery and application of novel ideas to real-world situations. Most organizations need more innovations if they are to be high performers in a competitive environment.

Why can't everyone—custodians, telephone operators, shipping clerks, accountants, salespersons, engineers, factory workers—have two jobs the way managers do? Managers are expected to do their routine jobs and innovate. Why can't everyone have a similar job description?

Sounds simple, doesn't it? Can you visualize the slogan "Everyone an innovator"? But if tomorrow every foreman, supervisor, middle manager, and top-level executive in an organization turned to his or her staff and said, "Starting today you will have two jobs—your routine one and innovation," what do you think would happen? Not much! In fact, there might be chaos.

The idea that people who actually do a job are experts at their job (more so than their boss) and that these experts have creative and analytical capabilities that they are not using is neither novel nor hard to prove. Each one of us has a Porsche mind, but we tend to perform like a poorly tuned 1978 Fiesta with its handbrake on.

How can we learn to release our brakes and step on the gas? What is it that is keeping you and me and everyone else from finding creative solutions to work-related problems? Research over the last 30 years has identified four major impediments—none of which is surprising. In fact, I often ask people in my workshops to form small groups and list what they think are the major brakes holding back their Porsche mental engines. They always list the same ones.

1. *Lack of Incentive.* "Why should I generate new ideas? How will I benefit from this? What has my boss told me in the past when I suggested changing something? Why struggle to overcome inertia? There is no payout in it, is there?"

2. *Lack of Skills.* "For years," thinks the employee, "I have done what my boss told me to do, and before that I did what my teachers told me to do. Now I am being asked to do something I have never done—or not done very often. I don't know anything about creative problem-solving. I also have never had any experience in presenting ideas to management. I need to learn new skills and I need the chance to practice them."

3. *Lack of Time.* "Assuming I have the right environment and I know how to identify problems and discover creative solutions, *when* am I supposed to do this? When do I have the time?"

4. *Fear.* "Even if I have the time, skill, and incentive, I'm not sure I want to go out on a limb and present my ideas before a crowd. They may laugh. I'm afraid to fail."

Fear can be a powerful inhibitor. I learned that when I was in the fifth grade at LeMoyne School in Chicago.

One day, when my teacher, Miss Sykes, was droning on about astronomy, something extraordinary happened.

Leslie, the boy sitting behind me, raised his hand. Why was that so special? Leslie never raised his hand—ever. He was the smallest kid in the class and the oldest. He had flunked three times, had terrible teeth, little pig eyes, bad breath, and a scrawny uncoordinated body.

"Miss Sykes! Miss Sykes!" Leslie shouted out. "Miss Sykes, why is it that when I look at the sun, I sneeze?"

My eyes opened wide. Snap! I was alert and waiting for the answer. Holding a silly underinflated, multicolored beachball that was supposed to represent the sun, Miss Sykes looked at Leslie with wide-eyed incredulity and then turned her head to the side. She was trying hard to hold back a laugh. She couldn't. Everyone exploded. There were howls of laughter, hoots, and backslapping—even tears. Finally, Miss Sykes settled the class down and said, "Thank you, Leslie"—and promptly went back to her lesson on planets, moons, and stars.

I was enraged. First of all, I thought Leslie had a great question. I sneezed when I looked up at the sun, too. "Maybe," I thought, "science has some use after all." But I did not learn the answer that day, and I still sneeze when I look up at the sun.

But the lesson that was indelibly tattooed on my psyche that day resulted from the laughter and jeers of my classmates and of my favorite teacher. What could be more humiliating? Or fearsome?

After this experience, I only talked in grade-school and high-school classes if I were called on. I never raised my hand or asked a question—not once. I learned to give other students I passed in the corridors a big smile as if I knew them, but I never talked at public meetings.

Today I teach college students and give lectures all over the country. I never flinch when I am introduced on the platform. In fact, I enjoy every second of it. But even to this day, when I am in the audience and have to stand up to introduce myself or ask a question of a speaker—even in a small group like a Sunday school class—my tongue thickens and my stomach knots. Fear of failure! Fear of derision! Leslie's ghost is still with me.

To release our brakes we need the help of leaders. Managers must develop an environment in which there is mutual trust—one in which a work group can laugh with one another, but never at anyone. Managers need to become coaches, teachers, and guides. They need to help the people who work with them learn the concepts and skills needed for problem solving, and the organization must reward teams for their efforts. However, many employees discover that the real reward is intrinsic. It comes from seeing an idea you were part of put into action.

"Everyone an innovator" is not a hollow slogan. The alternative is to limit an organization to the creative and intellectual talents of its managers. Even though these people may have immense ability and make heroic commitments, their organizations will have an increasingly difficult time surviving, let alone leading, in a competitive market where other organizations have learned to release the brakes. Why not use everyone's Porsche minds?

Trust Is Digital

Some things in life can be thought of as digital and others can best be understood as being analogue. For example, a second hand on a clock or the speedometer needle in an automobile are what mathematicians call analogue. They are continuous activities that can vary. A growing tree, a line drawn on a paper, or the sound of a plucked violin string are analogue events. You can have a little bit less of phenomena that are analogues—just think of a dimmer switch that controls a light.

A lightning bolt either occurs or it doesn't. A woman is either pregnant or she's not. A crystal goblet is either cracked or not cracked. Digital events are not a matter of a little bit more or a little less; they are either evident or not evident. There is no such thing as half a lightning bolt or being a little bit pregnant. A conventional light switch is either on or off.

Trust is digital. There is no such thing as almost trust or partial trust. You have it or you don't. Half trust is half doubt.

Other animals may be mutually interdependent and organize complicated societies with a division of labor, but their behavior is basically programmed. It is in their genes. Mutual trust among animals is not earned or learned. Bees, birds, and beavers perform and live in intricate complicated societies, but they are not based on what we humans call trust.

Trust is a purely human quality. So is distrust. Trust is an invisible lubricant. When it exists in an organization—a marriage, team, or business—each person has great freedom to act. People share common values and they have mutual respect for one another's feelings and thoughts.

What happens to an organization when trust, like a light switch, is turned off? The answer, if you stop and think about it, is predictable.

Olga Schonfield, manager of the notions department at a store in Chicago, had come to the U.S. in 1947. She was born into a venerable Hungarian family and was educated in music, literature, and languages. She survived Hitler's concentration camps, but, rather than becoming cynical and self-centered, she remained an extremely caring, gentle, and trusting person, despite this horrible experience.

She hired me to work as stock boy on Saturdays and Tuesday nights. I unpacked and arranged hundreds of items—threads, needles, snaps, patterns, scissors. I also assembled large cardboard storage closets. Because women (and men) in that era were modest, I also had the job of wrapping huge boxes of sanitary napkins in plain paper. I thought my job was a sissy one, and I was teased by the other employees of both sexes.

Olga was in her early fifties and I was sixteen when we met. She and her husband, Joe, had no children, and after a few weeks I realized that she was "adopting" me. She brought me small suppers, often foods I had never tasted—pickled beets, cold duck, red cabbage—and over these picnics on a card table in her small office, we learned a great deal about each other. She encouraged me to improve my grades and even set up a study table (her desk) for me when I had a chemistry test coming up, since she knew that I couldn't go to college if I failed chemistry. She met my parents and sisters, and by the time I was a senior in high school, we were special friends.

Olga was a firm and fair boss. She spent time coaching and encouraging everyone. Her department was tidy and her employees were attentive to customers. We were all proud of the fact that we had the best notions department in the city—at least we thought so.

But on a bitterly cold night in February, my friend and fellow employee, Jerry, and I were told that the owner's sons had taken over the management of the chain of stores and had instituted several policy changes. As we left the store at 9:45 p.m. on that Valentine's Day, we, along with every other employee, were stopped at the door and required to empty our pockets and show receipts for our packages. The new managers stood off to the side and glowered at us as two uniformed private policemen supervised this unannounced procedure.

I had purchased a box of note cards and a small silver pen in the store's stationery department and had surprised Olga with this Valentine gift. This created a problem, since Olga had no way of showing a receipt for these items. Having discovered these articles, the policemen made her empty her purse and then they went through the pockets of her coat.

Jerry and I looked through the window and saw Olga sobbing. She stood with several other employees near the fire door—humiliated and frightened.

Now Jerry was not an average teenager; he was anything but that. He was brilliant. His native intelligence was immense and his imagination was equally developed. He was the best math student at Senn High School, and he never studied. He knew how everything worked—motors, clocks, radios, atom bombs—and could repair anything. He also was fiercely independent, competitive, and highly combative when he believed there was an injustice being done.

Jerry told me he was declaring war on the store's management and wanted me to join in with him. I knew immediately and with certainty that if I had to pick sides—the power, wisdom, and wealth of the top manage-ment versus this impassioned pimply-faced teenager—there was no contest. Jerry would win. I agreed to help.

Olga's awkward situation was straightened out, but the working environment in the store changed. The "old" managers used to walk around and would get to know the employees. They even stepped in and waited on cus-tomers if the salespeople were busy. Once the new own-ers' father helped me wrap sanitary napkin boxes and we talked about Mel Torme and strawberry cheesecake. A few days later he came by and thanked me for teaching him how to break heavy twine with his hands. The new man-agers installed mirrors and electronic bugs in storerooms and gave lie detector tests to new employees. Time clocks were placed on the third floor and we had to punch in and out for lunch breaks as well as beginning and ending times. In the past, our department managers had turned in our hours.

Being juvenile and self-righteous, Jerry and I thought of ourselves as Robin Hoods or Pancho Villas when we started our guerilla warfare. We took our coffee breaks in the basement and started swiping pies from the bakery and sharing them with the porters and cleaning ladies. Then our activities escalated. We sabotaged new washers and dryers in the appliance department. Jerry jammed the time clocks and, when they were repaired, he did it again and again. He knew how to spin the final sales total num-bers on the cash registers—I think with a magnet—thereby confusing the finance department. Fire alarms went off (Jerry's doing, I'm sure), and once he made a stink bomb by lighting a role of film and placed it inside a manager's office and then locked the door with liquid solder.

During this period Olga became ill and was hospitalized. Jerry escalated his activities. Once he asked me to help him move a large rubber raft. We wedged it in the revolving front entrance door in such a way that it obstructed traffic for hours. I decided to quit and a few months later, Jerry did, too. Olga came to my high-school graduation, but her health never returned; she died during my freshman year at Carleton College. Jerry went on to a brilliant academic career at MIT and Harvard. The last I heard he was a vice president of a major corporation.

The department store we worked at, a major force in Chicago merchandising for decades, went out of business. It took several years for the final demise, but I know when the seeds of destruction were sown.

It came as no surprise to me that when Robert Levering and Milton Moskowitz, authors of *The 100 Best Companies to Work for in America*, did in-depth studies of the "best of the best"—twenty firms they call great places to work—that there was no combination of benefits (pay, profit-sharing, medical plans, free lunches, etc.) that could overcome deep-rooted rivalries and distrust between workers and managers. Just as love characterizes the attitude of both parties in a good marriage, trust characterizes the attitude of both sides in a good employment relationship.

Levering and Moskowitz found that trust was completely lacking in bad places to work, appeared sporadically in workplaces considered mediocre, and was the cornerstone of every great place to work. You may want to challenge their list, which includes such firms as Fisher-Price Toys, Northwestern Mutual Insurance, Publix Supermarkets in Miami, Apple Computers, Hallmark Cards,

Delta Airlines, Federal Express, Gore, 3M, Marion Labs, and Pitney Bowes. There are many other great places to work, but their research, which involved hundreds of interviews with employees—clerks, production workers, and salespeople both on and off the job—supports the fundamental importance of trust as a prerequisite for excellence.

Trust cannot be bought or sold. It cannot be freeze-dried or put in little envelopes. Trust is earned. And when it exists, it creates an environment where people feel free to try new ideas, to risk, to venture, to disagree, and to fail. High-performing companies do not develop a trusting environment because it is good for business. They do it because it is good to do—period. A company that has a soul and a heart can be a hard-nosed and demanding place to work. There are many ways to be a good parent, a good teacher, a good coach, or a good employer. But without trust no one can enlist others to give their best. Trust is digital.

The Only Star System That Works

There is only one star system that works to improve team productivity. And that system is not the one that most organizations choose to use.

How do you feel when one or two other persons are picked out of your group and called "stars"?

I used to return student exams arranged from lowest to highest so that I could examine the grade distribution. This meant that when the papers were returned, everyone knew who did poorly. The students handed the first papers—and I used to make a big fuss over the top performers—were the "stars."

It took me 20 years to recognize how demotivating this behavior was to most of the people in my class and, furthermore, that the top students didn't particularly like being singled out, at least not publicly.

Most of us do not like discriminating comparisons. In our own minds we see ourselves as able and industrious. We know that there is a star inside us.

I played football and basketball in college and was equally poor in both sports. But in those days there was no cutting, and I gave them my best effort and enjoyed the exercise, fraternity, and competition. I also learned an enduring lesson.

The basketball coach had a different philosophy than the football coach. The basketball coach believed in the star system. Three outstanding players were given special privileges, praise, and recognition.

The six of us on the "skin team" never articulated our feelings, but we knew that we worked as hard as anyone at the practice sessions and only got to play a few minutes, if at all. We felt like supernumeraries. We were practice fodder for the team members who really counted. We did not have good team spirit and the "stars" often squabbled among themselves. Our record was fair.

Walter Haas, the football coach, had a different philosophy. Haas and his associates believed that everyone was a star, that every person on that team had a strength that the group needed to multiply its energies.

This philosophy was not hollow rah-rah rhetoric. Wally Haas asked each one of us to meet his rigorous practice requirements. There were no exceptions. He reminded everyone that the game of football was a team game. And the sharp performance demonstrated by the first string reflected the hard work and determination of the second and third teams. No person stood alone. We were interwoven and interdependent.

What do you think was the attitude and motivation of this team? In 1954 Haas coached and motivated a team of mostly average players to a perfect season, one of the few in the nation.

Japan uses work groups and quality circles to produce cost-reduction ideas. The average worker at the typical Mazda factory produces some forty usable ideas a year. What most people don't know is that there are no names attached to those ideas. The group produces the idea—not the individual. Furthermore, there are no group bonuses; the bonuses belong to the whole organization.

But aren't Americans more individualistic? Don't we yearn for individual monetary awards even if we are members of a team? This is an open question.

Eleven years ago, I did a study on 100 idea-producing employees in the furniture industry. My objective was to help management design effective individual rewards for idea-producing employees. Both hourly workers and middle managers were interviewed. All these people worked with firms that had a history of worker participation and profit-sharing under a system called the Scanlon Plan.

My research findings surprised me and top management. The vast majority of employees—95 percent—did not want individual monetary awards. They did not think it was necessary. For example, one engineer I interviewed had saved the company $500,000 through a new inventory system. He told me this was his job and he didn't expect any individual award. Of course, he liked the recognition and was eager for advancement. Idea-producing employees liked the idea of the boss taking them out for lunch or sending them personal notes. Virtually all of the idea producers I talked with believed that seeing their ideas in action was a rewarding and motivating experience. The companies I studied decided not to initiate any individual reward system, such as the one used at that time by Ford Motors, which gave a fraction of the provable savings as a cash bonus.

Centenary College of Louisiana is an interesting case study. Most of the professors will voluntarily pick up the teaching loads of sick colleagues, visit with drop-in parents, come in on off-hours to see prospective students, take on coaching assignments, and help students over vacation periods. They will spend hours on new curricular revisions and on entertaining guest lecturers. Most nonteaching staff members at Centenary behave in the same way. There is no expectation of a bonus. A faculty member's name is never attached to an innovative curricular project or a major policy study.

Why do the faculty members behave this way? The reason is they do not feel like employees. They do not feel like interchangeable parts; they do not feel powerless. They feel like they are part of a team, a team with a worthy mission. They believe that the rewards of doing the right things for the right reasons are immense—but they do not expect material rewards or want or need individual applause.

Highly motivated individuals need rewards, recognition, and responsibility. But most of all, each of us needs to be needed. We need to know that each one of us is a "star," and that our contributions—our best efforts—are valued.

After her first day in first grade, my daughter Pamela came home and said, "Dad, my teacher told me I was like the center of an apple. Here, cut this apple in half and see."

I started to cut the apple as most people would—vertically—and she said, "Cut it the right way" (horizontally). Sure enough, when the apple was halved "the right way," there was a star in the center. What a way to start your school career!

Every one of us is in some ways a star. Managers who believe this and behave accordingly know that this is the only star system that works.

5

Ideas That Work

A while back, I received a brochure from one of the leading graduate schools of business. Its eye-catching graphics invited seasoned MBA's to return to the campus for a three-day workshop that would teach practical ideas to help them be more effective in their jobs. There would be no complicated theories, no mathematical models, no academic articles to read; rather, the participants would be told of ideas and concepts that successful managers actually use. All the ideas were simple, but these simple ideas could pay off big.

Two thoughts struck me as I examined that brochure. First, I thought, "Bully for you! Why not be up-front about sharing practical, relevant ideas that work?" But then I thought, "Why is it that MBA's who spend 2 years studying management at a cost of over $50,000 have to pay for a workshop to learn the real practical stuff? Why weren't they taught these things in their MBA program?" I still don't know the answer.

What I do know is that most successful managers don't look to complex theories when they make decisions. They don't spend hours studying decision trees or capital asset models. Most managers will tell you that their main concern is people.

It's relatively easy to manage computers, inventories, and money. It's difficult to manage colleagues, employees, and customers. Moreover, it's not enough to have satisfied customers and workers. The goal is to have enthusiastic and committed customers and workers. What can a leader—a coach, teacher, manager, or director—do to elicit that enthusiasm and commitment?

Leaders need more than good intentions. They also need tools. The techniques described in this chapter are not found in traditional textbooks. They come from experiences in ice-cream stores and supermarkets, from auto dealers and magicians, and even from Dr. Seuss. Deceptively simple, they work.

The Listening Lever

How do you feel when you approach someone—your boss, colleague, or spouse—with an idea and that person doesn't listen? How do you feel when someone gives you his or her full attention and actively listens without passing judgment?

Over the last decade, I've asked managers around the country, as well as secretaries, salespeople, nurses, postal workers, ministers, teachers, teenagers, accountants, engineers, and convicts, those two questions. The responses I get, which are listed on the next page, are always the same.

HOW DO YOU FEEL WHEN A PERSON...	
DOESN'T LISTEN?	**LISTENS?**
Stupid	Surprised
Angry	Good
Small	Great
Unimportant	Stimulated
Insignificant	Energized
Useless	Important
Dumb	Happy
Embarrassed	Special
Inconsequential	Significant
Not Valued	Appreciated
Rejected	Valued
Demotivated	Highly Motivated

Empathetic listening is not just a courtesy, it is a strong motivational tool. By using a tool, such as a lever, you can lift heavier weights than you can by using just your hands. The listening lever works the same way.

What are superiors saying to employees when they actively listen? Aren't they saying that they value their input, and that they look on them as bright, creative adults who are interested in improving the organization? Aren't they saying, "You are a needed and important member of the team"? Aren't they saying that the employees know more about their jobs than the supervisors do?

When was the last time someone really listened when you tried to articulate an idea that wasn't perfectly clear in your mind, but that you felt had great potential value? I'll bet that you're either having a hard time recalling such an occasion, or that if you can recall such an experience, you're doing so with great relish, because it was such a rare and memorable event. We all know, however, how infuriating it is to be ignored.

I remember how frustrating it was trying to explain the listening lever concept to my family at the dinner table. I was excited about this insight, but had not thoroughly thought out the details. As I started to explain it, I was interrupted by my son David who wanted to relate an incident that had occurred that day. I started again, and the phone rang.

After this second interruption, I tried again, only to find that no one was interested in the listening lever. Like a spoiled child, I lost my temper and bent my fork. "Won't anyone listen to my idea on the power of listening?" I blurted out.

In retrospect, I think I should have practiced what I had wanted to preach and done a better job of listening to what the others wanted to say.

The greatest potential for reducing costs and improving the quality of service of any organization is in the minds of ordinary people. But only a few organizations have tapped this valuable resource; the vast majority waste it. *The listening lever is one way to mine those precious minds of employees.*

Some managers think they prove they're listening by putting up a suggestion box. Their intention is good, but it takes much more to get listening leverage. Other managers think that because they tell everyone their door is always open they'll get a free flow of ideas. Generally, this isn't the case.

Participative management systems come in dozens of models, but the one thing they have in common is the expectation that all employees—shop workers, secretaries, accountants, customer service personnel—are to contribute ideas. Quality circles, involvement teams, productivity partners, and work group meetings are some of the various vehicles for finding ways to release the productive and innovative ideas of all concerned. And these group efforts are only a few of the approaches used by high-performing organizations to develop active participation.

Although these techniques don't require new plants, equipment, or office space, they do require time to train, nurture, coach, guide, and cheer on managers at all levels so that they can learn the listening techniques they need to run these meetings and develop other programs. The management system must also recognize and reward groups and individuals that contribute. Productivity, quality, and service become everyone's—not just the manager's—goal.

Admittedly, the listening lever doesn't always work. But when it does, the results are extraordinary. On average, Mazda factory workers come up with at least forty product improvement or work simplification ideas a year; most employees in American firms don't average one. The Herman Miller Corporation in Michigan and Scott Bader in England get even more ideas from their employees than Mazda. The listening lever, you see, isn't limited by geography or culture.

How would you like to work at a hospital, school, or factory where you're told you have two jobs? The first is to do your assigned task extremely well—for example, write computer programs, teach, assemble components—while the other is to work with others in your group to find ways to improve the quality and reduce the cost of your product or service. You're told that your ideas are needed so your organization can be in the vanguard of its market. Isn't this motivating? Don't you want to be part of an organization that aspires to be the best at what it does?

The listening lever concept also works with suppliers. Who better than your suppliers know what's going on in your industry, what the competition is doing, or what technological breakthroughs are imminent? By actively listening to suppliers, you motivate them to help you. In a decade, several companies—Chaparral Steel in Texas and A.J. Weller in Louisiana, among them—have grown into dominant forces in their markets by listening to their suppliers and, thereby, finding specialized market targets.

Finally, *the listening lever can help you improve customer relations.* Unless they're specifically asked, customers seldom go out of their way to say what they think of a particular product or service. Why should they? Instead, they vote with their feet.

A few years ago, I conducted a market study for a Michigan bank in which I asked both customers and non-customers to select the words they felt described the bank's behavior and image. I gave the same survey to the bank managers and board members. The managers believed that they were close to their customers and had a good fix on them. They thought customers perceived the bank as innovative, pioneering, sensitive, and dependable, and as being a good community citizen.

Surprise! A vast majority of both customers and non-customers thought that the bank was stodgy, self-serving, insensitive to customers, and indifferent to community needs. Customers also were upset with a new program that the bank had summarily instituted, whereby formally free checking accounts to nonprofit groups were stopped, and the hours of service were reduced. Furthermore, customers thought that the bank's methods for communicating its new policies were offensive and high-handed.

Much to the credit of the bank's management, they invited 120 people, a dozen at a time, to a luncheon-cum-gripe session in the bank boardroom. The managers did not try to defend or explain their position; they just listened to and recorded the customers' suggestions and complaints. The result of this encounter was that most of the people invited to participate in the meetings became vocal supporters of the bank, even though only a few of their ideas were implemented.

Though not a panacea, the listening lever can help you uncover problems and come up with solutions that you ordinarily might overlook. In both business and personal settings, it can help build commitment, loyalty, and enthusiasm. Just ask and see.

Positive Discontent

Administration is not the same thing as leadership. Colleges of business teach administration. The world needs good administrators, but it also needs good leaders. And we need these leaders serving on all levels of every human organization.

Some managers think it is their job to be problem solvers. In fact, they take pride in their ability to get to the bottom of things quickly and clean up the mess. Sometimes they solve the problem through their technical skills and knowledge, and sometimes they do it through their take-charge ability.

Whose heart doesn't palpitate to the hoofbeats of the great horse Silver when we know he is carrying the Lone

Ranger to the rescue? And who isn't struck by the cool, correct analyses of Mr. Spock from Star Trek?

While both these styles are certainly admirable in special situations, they are not the traits that modern managers need to develop premier organizations. Managers have a higher calling. Rather than problem solvers, managers should be problem finders.

Problem finding generally is not taught in college. This is unfortunate, since it is a skill that, like swimming and computer programming, can be learned. Business schools tend to specialize in problem-solving techniques, which are much easier to teach. But in our professional or personal lives, the real problem often is that we can't perceive the problem.

Problem finding is the necessary but not sufficient condition for entrepreneurship. And entrepreneurship and innovation are needed today, not only in business but in trade unions, education, medical service, religious organizations, and government at all levels. Problem finding is the flip side of opportunity finding.

If you think about it, virtually all improvements in medicine, technology, communications, and economic well-being have come about because someone was dissatisfied with an existing condition.

Virginia Shehee, Jim Montgomery, and Judd Tooke were not satisfied with the musical performance facilities in their town. These individuals were dogged in their effort to restore the local theater. They refused to be turned down. They got others to push with them, and, as a result, the town got a marvelous opera house in 1986.

I have seen single individuals on three different faculties stand up for what they thought was a better system of instruction. Others joined them and in a surprisingly short time, each college changed its curriculum.

Some people believe that if they are unhappy with a particular policy, product, or process associated with their job, they are just being negative and their boss won't like their attitude. Many bosses, in fact, do see employee dissatisfaction as destructive carping. But seeing a problem where others see none is a way of thinking that should be rewarded.

There is a big difference between a negative person who finds warts and a constructive person who wants the organization to do better. The paradox is that the most satisfied workers in American industry are those who are not content—not satisfied—with either their own work or their department's behavior. They are proud of their companies and their associates, but there is still a sense of things not being quite good enough. Isn't this the same outlook shared by high-performing musicians, athletes, and surgeons?

Federal Express and the 3M Corporation are modern marvels. Their management is respected worldwide. How do they continue to grow and sustain individual commitment at all levels? Both companies see discontentment as a positive factor, so long as the protesters take responsibility for their ideas and keep the discussion in the family. Like many Japanese corporations, they encourage all employees, not just managers, to help the company cut costs and improve quality.

But the courage to disagree, protest, and put pressure on the powers that be doesn't always produce positive outcomes. Hitler and a small clique of fanatics effected a major change in their world that seems incomprehensible today. There are always people who, with great personal conviction, stand for ideas that, if put into effect, would be counterproductive or even destructive. The road to hell is paved with good intentions.

Thirty years ago I was part of the marketing department at a starch and refining company in Indiana. Within a week, I witnessed a bright young chemist convince a small group of technically minded production managers—who, in turn, convinced the executive committee—to drop one of their standard products, burnt sugar, and pursue and promote a new chemical, which was used in the machines that washed returnable glass bottles.

A year later, aluminum cans starting replacing returnable bottles and paper milk cartons grew in popularity. The new product was a flop. And the burnt sugar product that had been sold became a money machine for its new owners. Burnt sugar, or caramel coloring, is what gives cola, chocolate ice cream, and rye bread most of their brown color.

Changing course is not always a good thing to do. The change must be in the right direction. This is leadership—the moral courage to stand up and point out a new course and the vision to select the right destination.

Leadership—courage and vision—is not the exclusive property of great leaders like Winston Churchill. Each one of us—accountants, salespeople, teachers, production workers—can make the difference by exerting leadership in our own domain. The next time you sit in your Sunday school class or PTA meeting, look around your office or plant, or attend a trade show or conference, ask yourself, "Is this really good enough?"

Are You a One-Flavor Manager?

Sarah Necomb, a British college student, arrived in Shreve-port, Louisiana, on a hot and humid evening in mid-August. She and my daughter Jan had become friends in 1981 when my family accompanied me on a sabbatical leave to Bath, England.

Eager to give her friend a true picture of American life and of the South in particular, Jan took Sarah around town. Eventually, they decided to stop at a popular ice cream shop.

The girls ordered double dip vanilla and chocolate cones and a pint of ice cream—vanilla and chocolate—to take home. But the salesperson would not sell them a hand-packed pint with two flavors. The ice cream shop's policy was one flavor per pint. The young women were told that scooping out more than one flavor for a pint order slowed down their production process.

This logic puzzled them. What was the difference between two flavors on a cone, which the shop served, and two flavors in a pint container? They were so unhappy with the situation that they decided to forego the treat, and walked out of the store.

This kind of behavior—in which an organization arranges its terms of trade so to be favorable to managers or employees but not to customers—can be described as one-flavor management.

One-flavor organizations are common in communist countries. Why? Because managers in centralized socialist societies have different incentive systems than managers in free market economies.

Before the recent economic and political changes in the countries that made up the former Eastern bloc, plant managers were required to meet production quotas—and they sometimes resorted to bizarre tactics to do so. According to one account, when a Russian nail factory fell far short of its quota—which was stated in tons of nails shipped—the plant managers retooled their production and made one-ton nails. One-ton nails! Can you picture fifty flatbed train cars, each loaded with ten giant nails?

In another incident, described in the novel *Riding the Iron Rooster,* by Paul Theroux, which is about a train that traveled through Russia and China, burly attendants pulled passengers out of their beds at 4:00 a.m. so the attendants could remake the compartments before the train arrived in the station at 6:30 a.m.

We expect to find one-flavor managers and employees in areas of American society where there is government ownership and operation, and often we do. A few years back, when I lived in Holland, Michigan, a town of 50,000 people, the main post office was always crowded over the noon hour. Yet, half the windows were shut during this period because this was when half the employees took their lunch break.

I've asked small and large groups in different cities around the country, "How many of you have ever gone through a course registration procedure at a state college?" Hands shoot up. When I ask, "What did you think of it?" I hear lots of moans and laughter in reply—one-flavor management. Of course, I'm also guilty of one-flavor behavior when I schedule a required class at eight o'clock in the morning. This time suits me, but it clearly isn't the preference of most of my students.

Not long ago, I took three art posters to a large framing shop. The salesperson wrote out an order form and told me the posters would be ready in 2 weeks.

"Why so long?" I asked.

"Because we are busy," was the answer.

Three weeks later, when I called to find out if my posters were ready, I learned that work hadn't even been started on them. I was told that the shop had a large backlog of orders, which had been generated by a special promotion offered 4 weeks earlier.

When I finally went to pick up the framed posters, it took 2 hours to complete the transaction. One poster was framed incorrectly. When the estimated bill I had been given was recalculated, the salesperson discovered that the first clerk had made some mathematical errors. The final bill was more than $100 over the original estimate. The fellow who made the mistake, I was told, was just a coffee-break fill-in. He really didn't know anything. One-flavor management strikes again.

Contrast this with the experience I had when I stopped into a picture frame shop in New Orleans.

"How long will it take to frame a picture?" I asked.

"Three or four hours," was the reply.

"Three or four hours?" I asked in surprise.

The clerk took my tone and expression to mean that I thought the service wasn't good enough. "If you need it faster than that," he said, "I can do it in an hour or so, and, if you like, I'll take it over to your hotel."

We can find more one-flavor management in most doctors' offices, which are arranged so that the visiting process is easy for the doctor. Usually patients wait in a lobby or reception area and then are taken to a small room where they're often left to feel like a widget in the production line of a job order shop. A nurse comes in and preps the patient. Then, after another wait, the patient is hurriedly seen by the busy doctor.

I think that patients ought to be paid at least $5 if they have to wait over 5 minutes for a doctor. If that seems like an odd idea, you should know that this is exactly what Bank of America does at every one of its thousands of branches in California to make sure bank clients don't have to wait too long for service.

Government agencies have few reasons to change. But firms that operate in the private sector will find that, unless they have some special monopoly franchise, competition will punish their one-flavor behavior.

One reason Wal-Mart is outdistancing K-Mart is because of the superior performance of its store clerks. Last time I was in a Wal-Mart, I asked an empoyee if he could help me find a vacuum cleaner bag. He had just started climbing a ladder in order to change a light bulb, but he literally jumped off the ladder and greeted me with a smile. His courtesy and attentiveness seemed noteworthy, and it is—precisely because we have become accustomed to and tolerant of one-flavor behavior.

Carolyn Natenstedt has no title. She is a Jane-of-all-trades at a company in Shreveport. This firm specializes in industrial maintenance, but it also supplies specialized parts. One of her responsibilities is to deal with customers over the phone.

One day, a new customer called her and asked if he could have a 4-foot piece of specialty steel. Like lumber, steel comes in standard lengths. The other firms would sell a 4-foot piece of steel, but they wanted to charge the customer for a full 12-foot length of pipe.

Carolyn told the customer that they would cut the steel, deliver it, and charge only for the 4 feet. Customers who want 4-foot steel, she told me, deserve the same quality and treatment as do major accounts. Is it any wonder that A.J. Weller has doubled in sales each year for the past 6 years of its existence?

Over the long haul, organizations must do two things: They must sense and serve the needs of their customers and, at the same time, meet long-term profit requirements. One-flavor organizations have lost sight of their reason for being—service to their customers. They have no long-term future.

In the end, the organization that goes the extra mile, stands by its products, emphasizes quality and reliability, and frequently monitors customer preferences has the best chance of not only surviving, but also of flourishing. Organizations must change their ways or pay the costs. One-flavor management is not the wave of the future.

Keeping Your Customers

Years ago, when I did marketing studies for the S&H (Green Stamp) Corporation in New York, we used these studies to demonstrate the value to retailers of using trading stamps to attract new customers. As with other forms of sales promotion, not everyone would be influenced by them, but we could show that if the trading stamps would increase sales volume by even 2 percent, the additional net income generated by the stamps would justify the cost.

Focusing on the benefits derived from attracting new customers is a good idea. But in their eagerness to get new customers, some managers lose the old. The following incident illustrates my point.

"What do you think about bratwurst without sauerkraut?" asked my wife Lucy 5 years ago.

"Not so good," I responded. And so, on a rainy Friday at 6:30 p.m., I made a trip to the supermarket where we did a major share of our shopping.

I waited until the assistant manager finished his conversation with an attractive female employee before I asked him where I could find sauerkraut. I bought a large jar, which had the store's private label on it, and drove home.

My wife opened the jar and found some dark foreign particles in it. I was horrified. Back to the store I went to tell the manager my problem. He took my jar and told me to get another one. I picked one up and noticed the top was not on tight. A second was loose also. A third one seemed fine. As I walked to the car I decided to open the jar just to be sure.

This one had more black material in it than the first one. When I returned to the manager, he told me to try a different brand. Seeing no other large jars, I picked up two small cans of a nationally advertised brand and walked back to the manager's station in the front of the store. The manager did some calculations and told me that there would be an additional 13-cent charge. Pointing to a line of four people in the express checkout lane, he said, "You can pay over there."

Something snapped. It was now 7:00 p.m., and I was wet, cold, hungry, and irritated.

"You would think you would be bending over backward to be good to me. Just think about what would have happened if we got sick on your sauerkraut. What about all the other customers who could be hospitalized from this defective product? I probably saved you from a major lawsuit. I've spent 30 minutes on a simple errand and now you want me to stand in line." I tossed him a quarter and left.

My family initially thought I overreacted. But I disagreed. After all, I was an old customer. After talking it over, my family and I decided to stop shopping at that store. Over a 13-cent incident, that store lost thousands of dollars a year from us.

Just think of all the money that this supermarket probably spent on advertising and promotions to attract new customers. How much would this store pay for a new customer? Why not cherish and serve the old customer?

Contrast my story with an account that appeared in *The Wall Street Journal* a few years ago. An American living in Tokyo purchased a turbo-oven from a department store where she had shopped for several years. When she tried it out, she discovered there was no cooling fan attached to the motor. Impossible! How could this happen? Don't the Japanese pride themselves on zero defects?

She notified the store by phone. The next evening when she arrived home there were three people waiting for her in the lobby of her apartment building—the sales clerk, the appliance department manager, and the vice president of the store. They had come to deliver and install a new oven. They also brought her gifts—fruit, flowers, chocolates, and a gift certificate. "Would she, could she forgive them for this error?" they asked.

Stanley Marcus, a founder of Neiman-Marcus and one of the outstanding marketing people of this century, likes to tell the story of how his father treated a good customer who wanted to return an expensive gown, which she had apparently worn. His father generously gave her a refund, thanked her for her business, and apologized for any inconvenience. He told her he hoped they could serve her better in the future. "Why not confront her?" Stanley asked his father.

His father explained that this customer bought thousands and thousands of dollars' worth of merchandise, and so did her friends. It was worth a few hundred dollars to make her a happy and committed customer.

Centenary College of Louisiana has an unusual executive MBA program. Even though it is the most expensive program within 200 miles, it is oversubscribed. Each week, two to four people ask for applications, and the waiting list grows. Yet not one dollar has been spent on promotion. There are no fancy brochures or posters. There are no sales or admission representatives. But everyone connected with the program has their eyes on one thing—helping these mature, ambitious, self-motivated students succeed. After all, they are our customers. And because we have 160 loyal and committed students, we need not look for new customers. They seek us out.

Each of us is an important customer, for each of us can vote with our feet and our purses to be someone else's customer. Many organizations have satisfied customers. But this is not good enough. Many satisfied customers will shift allegiance over small incidents.

A 1988 study conducted by Burger King indicated that only 30 percent of the customers who defected to other fast-food restaurants did so because of price or quality of the food. The vast majority left because of inattentive or rude employees. The company discovered that a mere 5 percent increase in the retention of existing customers would double its net profit. Burger King introduced a program that allowed it to listen and respond quickly to customer complaints. Defections fell by more than 5 percent, and profits climbed.

Since people are willing to change their allegiance when they feel they have gotten less than they expected, why not aim to give customers more than they expect? Then you will have joyful customers—regardless of whether they are new or old.

How Not to Close a Sale

The Faulty Refrigerator

"Do you like the coppertone color or the white one?" A friendly appliance salesperson at a branch store of a national chain asked me this question almost 7 years ago. It was my job to buy a refrigerator for our new home before my family moved to town. Since I rarely purchase such big-ticket items, this was a memorable experience for me.

"Is the morning a better time for delivery than the afternoon?"

This salesperson moved me from being a casual browser to a purchaser in less than 20 minutes.

During the process of writing up the order the salesperson asked if I knew about the maintenance contract I could buy for this refrigerator. I told him I wasn't interested, and the topic was dropped—until after I signed the order.

"You really should consider our service contract, especially on your model, because you have an ice maker.

Everyone has trouble with ice makers. You'll probably get your money back on this alone."

A little irritated, I remarked, "Our previous refrigerator ran for 15 years and it only required one service call, and that was to change a belt. I assumed refrigerators had improved, not deteriorated, and, furthermore, if my model has known defects, I should have been told about this before I signed the order."

The refrigerator arrived with a long, ugly scratch on the door. The installation man told me I could have a $35 rebate for the scratch and that he would touch it up so that it would hardly show.

Then, before I could respond, he tried to sell me a service contract. Again I heard what a good deal it was. He told me about all the happy customers he knew personally. I told him that I wanted a perfect refrigerator—not a touched up one—and that I did not want a service contract. A few days later a courteous employee delivered another refrigerator. He also tried to sell me a service contract. I noticed that the interior light didn't come on when I opened the refrigerator door. He changed the bulb. A few weeks later the bulb, which was under warranty, burned out again, and a repairperson changed it. Once again, I was offered a service contract.

I received a phone call at my office from a store employee telling me it was not too late to buy a service contract. That same afternoon, my wife received a similar call at home. Enough was enough!

I wrote the president of the company and told him I was not happy with his sales approach. It is obvious, I wrote, that service contracts are profitable to the company, since everyone is trying to sell them. I noted, however, that there is absolutely no way a prudent person can know whether it is a good deal to buy a contract, since there is no performance data given to the customer. This is like placing a $200 bet without knowing the odds. Furthermore, I explained, most insurance experts believe it isn't economical to insure small risks; insurance is meant to cover large risks.

The corporate president didn't respond to my letter. However, a month or so later, his director of public relations sent me a letter in which he told me about the many people who are living at the very edge of their incomes and, without this insurance, their families wouldn't be able to have their appliances serviced. Of course, he missed the point. Is the service contract, in terms of rational insurance principles, a good deal for the average customer?

Except for a light bulb that continually shorts out and an ice maker that—like everyone else's—works imperfectly, our refrigerator has performed flawlessly. I like it. But I still don't like the way the sale was closed. Maybe it's just me.

Trick Closes

Four years ago, I was invited to a semiannual sales and management meeting of the A. J. Weller Corporation. Tom Edwards, the president, and his two partners had built a multimillion-dollar corporation from scratch in a few years. They are in the business of providing specialized maintenance service and parts to industrial firms across the country. It is a competitive business and they have earned the respect of large and small customers through quality and service.

I arrived at the meeting just as a video started. Beautifully produced, it was called *How to Close the Sale* and had received an award for the best training film of 1978.

The video presented ten tried-and-tested techniques for closing the sale. What made the film so fascinating was the manner in which the sales closing techniques were presented. In the script, a British salesperson, Richard Sullivan, is ruminating about why he isn't more successful. His sexy girlfriend, Tess Wyatt, drops into his apartment and there are now two stories going on. She is trying to seduce him—or at least interest him—but he wants to tell her about the ten ways a salesperson can get orders. The audience gets to look in and listen to these ten sales episodes, which are acted out with verve and humor.

Close one was Ask for It. This seems like good straightforward advice. You can imagine how Tess tried this approach on Richard. But Richard wanted to tell her about some really clever sales tricks he learned, such as close two. This is a ploy in which the shopper is presented with a question, which assumes he or she has already decided to buy the item. For example, the salesperson asks, "Would you like it in coppertone or white?" "Would you like the car headlights to flick off automatically or manually?" Either answer moves the customer toward a final commitment.

Close three was not memorable. But sales close four, the Half Nelson, was. Using this technique, you get an arm lock on the order by taking the client's questions and turning the answers into a vise-like hold. Here are some examples:

> *Customer:* "Will this car really get 32 miles to the gallon?"
> *Salesperson:* "If I can prove it, will you take it?"
> *Customer:* "Will this duplicating machine collate as fast as the Xerox machine?"
> *Salesperson:* "If it does, will you buy it?"

Bang! You got' em in a half nelson!

Sales close five is called The Duke of Wellington. Supposedly this is the system the Duke of Wellington used to make hard decisions. A list of positive points, *The Whys,* is written down by the customer and compared to the list of *Why Nots.* The salesperson is advised to help the customer come up with positive ideas, which should be recorded first on the left side of the page. Then, the salesperson can say, "Looks like the 'why nots' are really quite few. Shall I write the million-dollar policy?"

The Cautionary Tale, the sixth approach, and a variant of this closing technique, the seventh, were illustrated in the next vignette. Here, salespersons are told to tell a dramatic story of the dire things that happened to a person who didn't buy the life-insurance policy or machine that they're trying to sell.

Sales technique eight is a tactic a salesperson should use if the client is not buying. "Please accept my apology. I know I did something wrong. How do you think I should approach other customers?" The customer may help the salesperson and, in so doing, answer his own objections and sell himself.

If a customer says, "I want to think it over," you are encouraged to first agree with the customer and then move to the Process of Elimination, close nine. You ask questions that will get the customer to say "no." For example: "Is it the warranty that bothers you?"

"No."

"Is it the payment schedule?"

"No."

Finally, the customer says everything is fine or the real objection comes to light and then maybe you can get a Half Nelson on him or use the Duke of Wellington.

The video is fast-paced with Richard Sullivan playing three different roles—selling a piece of capital equipment, a car, and an insurance policy. In the end, his girlfriend overcomes his final objection (close ten, a combination approach) and they hug a little on the sofa.

How did the audience like the video? They burst into applause. It was well done. No doubt about it.

As I walked to the podium a few thoughts went through my mind. I knew many of the people in the room and I both liked and respected them. They were real professionals who took pride in their work. Yet, I felt uneasy. Maybe I remembered how the refrigerator salesperson had used some of those tricks on me.

In any case, my first question was, "How did you like the video?" Most people, but not everyone, applauded. They were in a good mood. "How many of you," I asked, "would want your spouse and children to watch you close a sale using the manipulative tricks in the video?" They looked at each other, thought for a few seconds, and the smiles left their faces.

I went on to remind them that their company was successful because it sensed and served the real needs of its customers better than most in its field. I reminded them that honesty, service, and integrity, not slick tricks, had made them prosper. Their heads nodded in agreement.

Who wants to be coerced, conned, tricked, or half nelsoned?

The Honest, Caring Close

One of the most successful realtors in the Midwest is a woman who didn't start selling houses until her husband died over 10 years ago.

Her approach is quite simple. When a client (a family moving into town, for example) contacts her, she arranges a one-hour listening session in her office or her home. She discusses the following types of issues with the family: How long do they think they will stay in the community? What do they do for recreation? How active are they in church or civic affairs? How do they like to entertain? What kind of hobbies—woodworking, gardening, reading, music—do the different members of the family enjoy? Her clients realize that she is trying to understand how they live their lives and what they might value in a house and a neighborhood.

Next, she spends time with her clients going over a large map of the community. She points out parks, shopping malls, libraries, schools, and churches. She helps her clients focus on a few neighborhoods that seem to meet their needs. Then, before they go look at houses, she shows them her inventory of homes and where they are located. She knows a great deal about most of the houses she is showing and is dead honest about them. If she has any doubts about a roof or sprinkler system, she makes note of it. She tries to show how space may be used or reorganized. She doesn't pressure people or push to close a sale.

Her clients make up their own minds. She attends the real estate closing; she is there when the family moves in; and she sustains the relationship through the family's adjustment period. Nothing fancy. No tricks or gimmicks.

A few years ago, Peter Cook, the owner of a Volkswagen dealership in Grand Rapids, Michigan, told me how he got the exclusive franchise to distribute Mazdas to other dealers in a three-state area. He was not the most sophisticated businessman or the wealthiest person who wanted the account. He, like the other suitors, made three or four trips to Japan. But unlike the others, he tried very hard to both learn and follow Japanese business and social customs. He is by nature a reserved and humble person who had developed a successful automobile business on the basis of honesty and service. No slick sales tricks are tolerated in his business. The Mazda executives in Japan knew this and they believed they could trust him.

What is it that we want from professional salespeople? We want them to listen hard to us as we try to articulate our needs. We want them to help us find solutions to our problems. We want to have long-term trusting relationships that go beyond contracts. We want them to be not a necessary evil, but a necessary good.

Doing Less Can Pay Off

Doing more by doing less is an idea that seems to have wide application. Here are some examples.

Why is it that so few students retain very much from their basic course in economics? Dr. Harold Christensen, a master classroom teacher, listened to my concerns.

Most of my students are conscientious. They read their assignments, do their homework, write papers, and study for exams. Yet how many—even of those who get good grades—have any long-term command of the concepts I try to teach them? Frequently they actually mix up ideas that they think they know cold. This phenomenon seems to be universal in economic teaching, and it often is found in other disciplines, such as chemistry or history.

The problem, Christensen explained, is with the instructor—in this case, me. "Look at a typical textbook in principles of economics. Look at all the topics you cover," he replied. "How can anyone comprehend, remember, and apply the hundreds of concepts you cover in 15 weeks?"

He's right. In fact, even after 25 years of teaching basic economics I find new insights or I discover that ideas that I thought I knew slipped away, or I didn't have them quite right.

Part of the answer to my problem is obvious. I am trying to do too much. Do you remember the movie *If It's Tuesday, This Must Be Belgium*? This silly film was about the exploits of a group of Americans on a quickie tour of Europe — basically changing currencies, buying souvenirs, and taking snapshots as their bus moved on.

A traveler typically can get more from a trip by concentrating on a few things. Those who really wanted to understand England, for example, would do well to focus on a few select places that make a lasting impression. Besides the standard sights, the smart traveler might climb up a hill in Somerset to see the famous chalk horses or walk through the glorious gardens of eighteenth-century Stourhead. The trick is to seek out places and situations where it's possible to meet the locals and talk with them one-on-one. In so doing, the traveler comes away knowing more by doing less. The same concept—doing more by doing less—works on an organizational level, too.

After I conducted a management workshop in Colorado, Jim Patterson, an entrepreneur who has a national reputation in the dry-cleaning industry, invited me to Emil-Lene's, a one-of-a-kind restaurant. We drove 3 miles out of town and then down a country lane past a prison to an unmarked gravel drive, and there it was: a cinder-block building with dozens of cars—trucks and motorcyles as well as Jaguars, Cadillacs, Fords, and Chevrolets—in the parking lot.

When we entered the restaurant, we were guided to our table. There were 124 seats in the two rooms and every one of them was occupied, and people were waiting for seats. There were people wearing cowboy hats and jeans; others were in three-piece suits.

What was the attraction? Certainly not the decor—cheap prints and dime-store pictures were on the walls. The sturdy wooden tables had no cloths.

A friendly waitress appeared and asked for our order. "May I have a menu?" I asked.

"No menus," she responded. "We have three things: a New York steak, a fillet, and baked duck."

"Three things—is that all you have?"

"No, sometimes we just have two steaks on the menu. The third item can change each day." We ordered fillets.

A huge 20-inch bowl filled with crisp raw vegetables was placed on the table. Next came a basket filled with three different kinds of homemade rolls. Then came a plate of spaghetti covered with a rich tasty mushroom and tomato sauce. After that, a fresh salad and a tiny ear of tender sweet corn accompanied the steaks, which were juicy and tasty. We raved about the food.

The swinging kitchen door opened and I saw iron skillets and a small charcoal grill. One of the helpers was dropping spaghetti into a 2-quart pot. It looked like my grandmother's kitchen. I had to find out more.

"How long has the cook worked here?" I asked.

"Twenty-four years—he owns the restaurant, but all of us are a team. I've been here 14 years. We help out and do different things. Today I helped with the corn and with the bread," the waitress told us with a sense of pride.

"Say, how does someone know what things cost if there is no menu?"

"If they ask, we tell them," she replied. "Would you like to try dessert?"

"What have you got today?"

"Same as every day—ice cream, homemade, vanilla."

"That's it?"

"You can pour a liqueur over it, if you like."

We did, and it was a memorable treat. In fact, the dinner, which cost us $20 each with drinks and tip, will never be forgotten.

How can a restaurant that can't be found without a detailed map and that serves only three entrees and one dessert survive in this modern world? How can a place like this, which doesn't advertise or use modern reservation techniques, not only make it, but flourish?

"This is a living case study," Patterson said, "of your concept of how less can be more." He was absolutely right.

There is a case to be made for adding to your product line. Isn't there an interest in new products and services? Don't you have to keep adding new features to stay competitive?

But there is also a danger. As organizations start to broaden their lines, they often lose quality. Why is this? Because few organizations can be equally good at all activities. The average quality frequently falls with breadth. International Harvester is a case in point. They tried to do too many things—refrigerators, stoves, industrial appliances—to the detriment of their traditional business.

Another example is academic curriculums found in most colleges. It is not unusual to find twenty-five to forty different majors or fields of study at a large university. Smaller colleges pride themselves on the hundreds of courses they offer. But possibly up to 80 percent of these courses are add ons whose quality is modest. Most high-performing schools, colleges, and universities could do well by reducing their offerings to the significant few, reducing majors, and concentrating on being brilliant in just a few areas.

Thunderbird, a unique university in Arizona, is committed to one thing—training businesspeople for overseas work. Its professors teach languages and business skills only at the graduate level. They do it very well, and their small menu of graduate courses attracts people from all over the world.

Violet Janks is a woman who, a decade ago at age 40, started her own small business in California. With very little capital and no experience, she opened a dry-cleaning operation.

Her location is halfway up a steep hill. It's hard to find. She knew she could not do all things well, but she could do one thing—treat every blouse, dress, shirt, or suit as though it were a valuable treasure to the owner.

She focuses on high-quality care, which requires a great deal of hand labor. Using a hospital approach, she set up an emergency room, an intensive care unit, and a recovery room. Garments are not put on wire hangers, but on wide frame hangers to preserve their shape. Each garment must meet high standards at every step in the cleaning process, "Equal," she says "to what I would want for my own most precious clothes."

Every new customer is given a tour of her operation and is shown what happens in this "hospital." Deviations from these standards—a flaw discovered in the garment—result in a handwritten note from Violet to the owner. She has a sustaining personal and professional relationship with hundreds of her customers.

Her plant does no drapes, carpets, or industrial garments. She sells no shoe polish, cleaning solutions, or fabrics. She and her staff of fifteen people do just one thing extremely well. And people pay a premium for it. In fact, they seek her out and ask to be a customer. Like the restaurant in Colorado, she has a waiting line of people from all income groups who want her unique service.

What is one thing your organization does extremely well? Could you do an even better job in this area if you eliminated some other activities? Could you do more by doing less?

Simple Ideas That Pack a Punch

Over the years, I've discovered some management principles that are not in traditional textbooks or management journals. They are simple ideas—simple but powerful.

What's Good About It? (Thumbs Up!)

While he was a professor of psychology at Purdue, Robert Schwarz taught me this principle. He explained that our critical facilities are so good that we want to immediately jump on an idea, analyze it, and point out the flaws.

This almost universal propensity has two undesirable consequences. First, it squelches creativity. Who wants to be jeered at or thought of as illogical? Second, once we commit ourselves, we tend to protect our own position.

For example, if someone suggests that a corporation should pay bonuses to factory workers who are not absent rather than punish those who are, one might say that's a silly approach. Once a commitment is made in our minds or spoken aloud, most of us find it difficult to change our stance. What would happen if, instead of focusing on the negative, we could find a way to let our minds walk around the proposal before we reject it?

Schwarz's approach of asking yourself "What's good about it?" is an effective way of converting our critical propensity to a positive, open-minded position. Not only do you suspend judgment, you actually seek out the good.

The principle works in all sorts of situations. For example, when you read a report or an article that seems flawed, try to find what is good about it. At a meeting when you hear what seems like a stupid idea—one that you tried before—or a half-baked idea, think to yourself, "What's good about it?" The next time you're in a meeting and someone suggests an idea, why not look up and say, "Let's explore that. What do you think might be good about this suggestion?"

Bob Schwarz had stationery and notepaper imprinted with a picture of a closed hand with the thumb pointed upward. I leave a piece of this notepaper on my conference table to remind me of the powerful principle he taught me.

A Hand-Written Thank You

A hand-written thank-you note can do more to motivate a person than most threats or bonuses. However, the thank-you note must be sincere, and the show of appreciation should come promptly.

Seems so simple and obvious, doesn't it? Yet, when was the last time your supervisor made a special effort to thank you for serving on a committee or taking on a special task? After each game, Vince Lombardi took time to shake hands and thank each player on his football team for their help—whether they played or not. He meant it. Their victories were always team victories.

A few years ago, I served on a community planning committee. We met for hours hammering out a proposal that was accepted. When the policies were approved by the town council, the mayor made no attempt to thank his committee members. We dispersed never to meet again. How do you think we felt?

What does a personal thank-you note say? Doesn't it say that someone recognizes you as a unique person and values your contribution? When was the last time you wrote a personal note to an employee or a new associate? A handwritten note—even of only one or two sentences—has long-term significance.

I Need You

Bob Wood was the plant manager of the Herman Miller plant in Bath, England, 10 years ago, when he told me how he came to work for the company. In 1975 Max Depree was vice president of the firm. He asked Bob to meet him in a hotel lobby in London, where he told him of his dream of developing an operation that would make office furniture as fine as any in all of Britain. But right now all he had was an old factory in Bath. He told Bob that the two of them would start from scratch, and that Bob would have to do everything at first. He would have no secretary or assistants, and the work would be long and hard. Furthermore, he would have to take a pay cut. Seems like a silly proposition to make to a successful young executive whom he had never met before and who had two small children and a large mortgage.

But Max said, "Bob, I believe you are the best I can find. With your talent we can make it happen. Bob, I need you." No one had ever said that to him before.

They shook hands and Bob took the job on the spot.

When was the last time you were told your organization needed you? Recently, I gave a talk to a group of forty managers. When I mentioned that one of our basic needs is the need to be needed, and that this human quality was a powerful motivating force, nearly everyone in the audience nodded in agreement.

Then I asked, "When was the last time you told your spouse that you really needed him or her—not for sex or to make dinner or to take out the garbage, but as the one person whom you most trust and need to make your life whole?" Two people had tears in their eyes. I don't know whether my words struck a chord because they hadn't said those words or because they craved to hear "I need you" said to them.

Modern management concepts and practices frequently are quite sophisticated and complex. Many of them are extremely useful. But some of us need to be reminded that the long-term success of any organization requires the voluntary commitment of men and women to give their best.

When used with integrity, simple ideas like *thumbs up*, a hand-written *thank-you* note, and *I need you* will motivate every one of us. Unlike pepper or garlic, these ideas can never be over-applied.

What's the Problem?

It never fails to fascinate me that when individuals are given the same facts, they discover different problems. This seems to be a universal human condition, and the results of this phenomenon can be disastrous.

In a management seminar I led at the Naval Management School in New Orleans, I gave the participants the following data:

> A textile firm in Georgia that specializes in making bath towels, had plant capacity to produce 100,000 towels a week. They were selling their towels under their own trademark to retailers all across North America.
>
> Since the recession they have been operating at 50 percent capacity, but even at this level they were at the break-even point. Their accountants told them that their variable or direct costs were constant at $7 a towel. The selling price was $9.
>
> This company was approached by a large department store chain. They asked the textile firm to manufacture a large order for them and put their store's label on the towels. They would pay $8 a

towel, which was less than the full cost but more than the direct cost.

A break-even graph was put on the blackboard. The groups were only told to talk about this information. They were not specifically asked to find a problem or suggest a solution. The following is an abbreviated summary of the groups' work.

Team 1: The problem is should the company take on this private label business, and the answer is clear. So long as the extra business makes a contribution to the overhead, the company should do it. Why not find more businesses like this?

Team 2: The problem is what to do about declining sales. They probably need a more aggressive sales effort, possibly some product improvements, and maybe a new advertising campaign.

Team 3: The problem is how to lower the break-even point. Is the plant antiquated? Is there too much staff? Are wages too high?

Team 4: The problem is what if existing customers find out that you are making the exact same product for a competitor? This could hurt you in the long run. Don't take on this business.

Team 5: There is no problem. Management can't change the business cycle. You should never consider taking on new business that doesn't cover the total cost. This is self-evident.

Team 6: The problem is a long-term strategic question. Should the company continue to make towels or does it have a comparative advantage in another line? What is going on in terms of consumer preferences, competition, and new markets?

Six teams of managers came up with six different ways of looking at the facts. Not one team was happy with just talking about the data. Each group perceived the problem differently and developed different strategies. Is it any wonder, then, that the profitability of competing firms in the same industry, from fast foods to commercial banking, differs so much?

One positive management lesson to learn from this example is that all of us tend to accept the definition of the problem too quickly. In each case, a team only took a few minutes to reach agreement on the problem. Usually some articulate, self-confident person presented his view, and the others concurred. Most of the time was spent in finding solutions and debating alternatives—none of which could be rejected or accepted since there was insufficient information. Does this happen in your office, around your dinner table, or in your boardroom?

When we all are sure we know what the problem is, there's a pretty good chance we are asking the wrong question. This may be caused by an erroneous, unchecked assumption, by a blind spot, or by a narrow perception of the problem. Sometimes we are really working on a symptom and not attacking the problem at all.

There is no quick fix for this common human condition—processing information too quickly and committing ourselves to work on what we think is the problem.

However, one practical approach that some managers have found effective is to separate the problem-solving process into three steps: (1) define the problem, (2) generate some solutions, and (3) analyze the solutions and select one of them.

The trick—and it is hard to do—is to force the group to define and redefine the problem in five different ways before you will discuss any suggestions. One manager told me that he calls this approach *walking around the situation*. By taking these walks, he frequently will get his associates to make U turns. Rather than asking for more salespeople, they examine their pricing policy; instead of buying new equipment, they contract out; instead of adding more quality-control personnel, they reduce the size of the quality-control staff but improve acceptance rates by other means. What's the real problem? This may be the most important question anyone can ask.

Back-Door Managing

Hoyt Yokem, the owner and manager of a car dealership, is a back-door manager. To see the ramifications of back-door thinking, we should first look at front-door managers.

A few years ago, a bright and enthusiastic 40-year-old man came to my office with an idea that he wanted me to help him develop. He wanted to improve the professional competence of health-care administration at all levels. His creative idea was to develop management modules, which he would market, and to provide closed-circuit instruction to his clients. He made contracts with five authorities in the field and was eager to get on the airwaves.

At our second meeting, I sensed disaster. This entrepreneur explained to me how he visualized being rich. He fantasized about his life of opulence. He was so certain that his venture would fly that he had images of opening his front door and having money pouring into the street.

This man was a front-door manager. Front-door managers have their eyes on the wrong things.

Profit is always derivative; that is, it's a return for taking risks and for providing services and products that are superior to others. The way to get high returns is not to concentrate on profits but on quality, service, and productivity.

Back-door managers have learned to sense what is important and to concentrate their efforts on those areas. For example, much of what is special about Japanese management is their almost fanatical concern with suppliers. Price enters into the negotiations, but paramount is the quality and dependability of goods and the ease of dealing with their suppliers.

What comes in the back door will determine how the cash register will ring over the long haul. Back-door managers frequently go against the stream of popular behavior. When everyone is trying the newest management techniques, they tend to focus on the basics.

One morning, while eating breakfast at Strawn's Restaurant in Shreveport, I overheard a telephone conversation that the owner's son was having with a supplier of fruits and vegetables.

The vendor was offering Florida strawberries of good quality at considerably lower price than the California berries that the restaurant usually purchased. The young man hesitated a second and then told the supplier that his father, Gus, was willing to pay the difference for the California berries.

If Gus were a front-door manager, he might think of ways to ever-so-slightly shave the quality of his famous strawberry pies. Who would know if he didn't start from scratch or use the finest ingredients? Gus knows that if he modernized his shop, replaced the tables, repaired the booths, and made the place look like a contemporary restaurant he wouldn't gain any customers. But if the consistently high quality of his strawberry pies fell by even 10 percent, there would be a profound negative reaction.

Car dealer Hoyt Yokem starts his day in the shop, not in the sales office. He meets with mechanics and parts people first. He knows the back end of the business and expects that quality repair work be done with high-quality parts. He expects repairs to be done right the first time. He expects every employee to treat customers and co-workers with dignity.

Yokem generally gets what he expects. His mechanics rarely leave him. They're committed to his company and like the idea that they have been instrumental in developing a reputation that keeps people coming to the front door.

Back-door managers do nothing fancy or magical. What they do looks simple: They concentrate on the three p's—people, products, and productivity. You could say back-door managing is a synonym for effective managing.

Numbers Don't Tell
the Whole Story

Some computers can do 10 million calculations a minute. Computers are great at processing information. Yet, no computer can recognize your face in a crowd, interpret a child's picture, or find an unmet need in the market. Since computers are mindless machines, they can never feel frustrated; they can never perceive a problem or conceive of a new idea. In short, computers cannot be entrepreneurs. Only creative men and women can be entrepreneurial.

Two young real-estate developers were kind enough to take me on a tour of the city when I first arrived in Shreveport three summers ago.

When we turned down Texas Street, I was struck by the view of the First Methodist Church. We drove past modern banks and office buildings and through an area of town called the Heights. Then we drove by some buildings that were being restored, and these two men started talking about what could be. Their imaginations were being sparked by each other. I lost interest in the tour and became fascinated with how the minds of entrepreneurs work.

A month later, I was taken on a similar tour, but this time by an accountant. This very bright person gave me a great deal of historical data about the city and specific buildings, and explained the tax implications of new construction projects.

These experiences made me think of how both ways of looking at the world are important: the historical, ordered world of the master accountant and the futuristic, fluid world of the entrepreneur.

Some managers, however, make a mistake when they think the accountant's data will give them sufficient information to make the right decisions. After all, numbers don't lie. But, financial accounting data are not really made for making management decisions. These data may be precise and orderly, but generally they're either incomplete or irrelevant. You must see through the accountant's numbers to make good judgments.

Assume that a bottle of beer is selling for $1. You go to the store and discover that it's having a sale, and you buy two bottles of beer for $1. The next day, the price is back to $1 per bottle. A neighbor you don't know asks if he can buy a bottle of beer from you. What do you charge him?

Cost accountants might tell you the beer is recorded on the books at 50 cents a bottle. An entrepreneur would not be concerned with book cost, but would want to know what the beer is worth today—the opportunity cost—before he sold it. In this case, the beer that cost 50 cents yesterday is worth $1 today. The accountant's record cost, though perfectly accurate, is entirely irrelevant to the final decision.

Given the following information, what should you do? Would you close down the Ajax book department?

AJAX DEPARTMENT STORE		
	Book Department	Toy Department
Total Income:	$10,000	$20,000
Direct Costs:	$8,000	$10,000
Overhead Costs:	$3,000	$4,000
Net profit/loss:	-$1,000	+$6,000

Your accountant may tell you that you might want to ignore the overhead cost, since it is an arbitrary allocation. But the answer to this management question can't be found in the historical accounting data. Although the numbers are correct, they don't tell the whole story. Nor can a fast computer help you. Ultimately only the subjective judgment of a human being can answer this question.

Think about this: It's possible that the book department is really a profit center. Maybe it's using space that isn't good for anything else. Maybe it's a source of traffic in the store—just as the night-club entertainers in Las Vegas are a source of traffic for the casinos.

This case is not completely fictitious. Marshall Fields in Chicago had such a situation 12 years ago. What did they do? Rather than close the bookstore, they boldly reduced the size of the toy department and remodeled and expanded the book department. Their approach paid off.

Accountants are valuable persons. Their skills are needed for tax and legal purposes. However, professional accountants would be the first ones to say that their accounting numbers are the starting point and must be studied and interpreted before they can be used.

Only the human mind can see beyond the numbers—see the fluid and uncertain possibilities that exist in the future. But not all subjective calculations are correct. That is why the free market is called a profit *and* loss system.

Management decisions require judgments about future events. That means that business will always be at least 50 percent art, and that the art of management celebrates what it means to be human. Computers can do 10 million calculations a minute, but they can't be creative managers.

No Strings Attached

After more than 30 years of study and reflection, I have come to three conclusions about management and human behavior.

First, when stripped to the bone, all the useful management principles I know are quite simple and easy to understand. Second, these principles are universal. They seem to work just as well in small organizations as large ones. They work in every type of organization—hospital, school, retail firm, bank, or manufacturing plant—and in all countries. Third, the simple, universal ideas that managers actually use are found rarely in management textbooks. But if they're not in books, how do people learn them? Sometimes from those closest to them.

My mother had to be one of the most extraordinary characters I've ever known, and my opinion is seconded by nearly everyone who ever knew her. She left school at age 13 and went to work at a notions counter in a dime store for $6 a week. All but 50 cents a week was used by her mother to pay for music lessons for her brother and sister. When she was 17 her stepfather died, and she supported the family. She had a fear of water, but learned to swim at age 50. She enrolled in a graduate literature course at the University of Chicago at 60, and even though she had no high-school or college background, she kept up with her classmates. She rarely intellectualized but instead listened to her heart. She and her friends gave more food, clothing, and household appliances to the poor people in our neighborhood than a small army of paid welfare workers.

She had an immense amount of energy. In an unselfrighteous way, she was an outspoken advocate for justice—not on a worldwide basis, but in day-to-day living with people who were hurting or left behind. She loved good food and stories and, most of all, she loved her children, Jessica, Laurel, and Barrie.

When I was 15 years old in Chicago, I started hanging out at the Uptown Boys' Club. Some of the toughest kids in the area used this facility for their gang headquarters, and I liked spending time with boys from the wrong side of the tracks. I found my new friends fascinating. They demonstrated a sense of mutual concern and brotherhood that I didn't find in my high-school clubs or athletic teams. They drank and smoked and, from time to time, got into trouble. I liked the adventure and romance, I suppose.

On a Friday night one April, two leaders of the Uptown Boys' Club invited me to go out with them. We drove to Swensen's Gas Station; I knew immediately what would happen. They broke a window at the back of the garage, entered the building, and in less than 5 minutes had loaded the trunk of the car with three boxes of candy bars, a case of soda, and some tools. We drove to a park and waited for the other fellows in the gang to meet us.

The police came first. We were taken to the police station and charged with theft—not only of the candy, soda, and tools, but also for a box of expensive cashmere sweaters, which was found in the car.

For some reason—possibly because my father was an attorney and involved in Chicago politics, or maybe because it was clear that I really didn't belong with the gang—the police officers segregated me from the others and, rather than locking me up, they drove me home.

You can imagine how I slept that night. The next morning, over a bowl of oatmeal, I told my mother the story. What did she do? What would you do if this were your son?

She got up, walked around the kitchen table, hugged her lanky adolescent son, and said, "I know you feel bad about last night, and I know you will do the right thing."

Here is a woman whose basic personality was as kinetic as a shaken bottle of ginger ale, a woman who could mourn for days over the death of a kitten or become ecstatic if you surprised her with a bunch of dandelions, calmly accepting the news of my escapade. There were no speeches, no wails, no evaluations, no sermons, no laying out of options, no threats, no punishments—just a hug and an assurance that she knew I would do the right thing.

That same morning I sold the shotgun my brother-in-law John had given me and pawned a WWII souvenir knife. I walked into Swensen's garage that afternoon, looked him in the eye, and told him I was part of the gang that broke into his garage. I gave him all the money

I had, which totaled $33, and told him I would wash cars on Thursday and Saturday afternoons to make up the difference.

During lunch at school on Monday, I told the boys in the club I was out and although I liked them and respected their street smarts, I didn't want to end up in jail.

My mother never told my father about my run-in with the law. She never asked me what I did about the situation, and I didn't tell her until I was out of college.

I got an entirely different reaction from her, however, the summer I was 19 and on break from college. Leaning back in an old wooden chair on the porch of our summer home, I let out a sigh.

"What's wrong with you?" asked my mother as she stood with two bamboo rakes in her hand.

A freshman girl I had really fallen for had dropped me, and I was mopey and whiney and feeling very sorry for myself.

"God, I hurt," I said. "I feel so unhappy."

What did my mother do? She kicked one of the legs of the chair I was sitting in, sending me crashing to the floor. My head knocked against the porch swing. She stood over me, her eyes dark and her teeth clenched, and with her index finger jabbing down at me she said, "Unhappy? Unhappy? Who ever told you God put you on earth to be happy? Happiness is a bonus. It's an unusual event. You're here to use your strength and mind to help others. Now get up and help our family. Start raking—now!"

Ten years later when I was a professor at Bethany College in West Virginia, one of my friends spent several hours with my mother during one of her visits. "Your mother gives more compliments and finds more good things to say about everyone and everything than anyone I have ever known. Is she always like that? Is she for real?"

"The answer to both questions," I said, "is yes."

You know how most of us give compliments: "Your talk was great, but it could have been shorter."; "You did a good job with that difficult customer, now see if you can keep from falling back into your old habits"; "Our parts came in on time with no defects—what a surprise"; or "Your term paper is provocative. Now if only..." My mother's compliments never had an if, and, or but attached.

Plato thought eternal truths exist in this world and that with proper guidance anyone would be able to recognize these principles in the same way we somehow are equipped to sense geometric relationships. I think Plato was right—at least to the extent that most of us can find valid and powerful insights for productive living in parables, in poetry, and in our relationships with special people—like our mothers.

So here are three simple but useful ideas that aren't found in sophisticated journals or textbooks: (1) Stop judging and haranguing one another and, instead, let others know you believe in them and trust they will do the right thing, (2) Remind yourself that life is an opportunity to make a small but meaningful difference in the lives of others, and (3) Give someone an honest compliment with no strings attached.

People like my mother give the rest of us a glimpse of what it means to live a good life—one lived with integrity, moral courage, zest, and humility. I believe that if there were a jury made up of Buddha, Confucius, King Solomon, Jesus of Nazareth, and Mother Teresa, the members would all come to the same conclusion about my mother's life. They would shout in unison, "Well done, Rose, well done!"

What Do You Do With Shirkers?

One of my all-time favorite children's stories is *Horton Hears a Who*. If you haven't read this Dr. Seuss book, you've missed not only a delightfully told tale encouraging kindness, tolerance, and compassion, but also a clear and memorable presentation of some powerful management principles.

Horton is an elephant with large ears that enable him to hear sounds other animals cannot. One day, Horton hears a call for help from a flower. There on the flower is a tiny speck, and on that speck is a whole village—Whoville—where thousands of microscopic people live out their lives. A disaster occurs and people call for help. Only Horton can hear them, and when he tries to explain the situation to the know-it-all monkeys who are in charge of the jungle society, they make fun of him.

Horton asks the mayor of Whoville to get everyone in the city to make noise—yell, beat drums, blow horns, whatever—to create enough noise so that the skeptical monkeys will know they are there. Everyone hoots and hollers and bangs and clangs, but the monkeys cannot hear anything. Horton desperately asks the mayor to search the city and see if there are any shirkers. Sure enough, he finds one little shirker hiding in a corner. The shirker joins in and, with his extra effort, raises the decibel level ever so slightly but enough for the monkeys to hear. Yes, there are little people in the jungle who need help. Horton is not crazy, and, of course, the monkeys will help protect the denizens of Whoville.

Twenty-five years ago, Craig, my then 5-year-old son, came to me with an old alarm clock that he had taken apart. "Dad," he asked, "which of these wheels makes the hands turn?" I had to explain to him that every gear—large and small—must be meshed properly to have the hands turn. There can be no shirking gears in a clock.

In human organizations of all sizes and types—hospitals, schools, restaurants, factories, banks—there are shirkers. Yet, unlike the alarm clock, these organizations will operate. But their level of operation will be lower than it would be if everyone could be persuaded to give his or her best effort.

The difference may be relatively small, but in the competitive world in which we live, almost all decisions are made on the basis of small differences. Many people will change hair stylists, auto repair shops, stockbrokers, retail stores, banks, or hospitals for a perceived small difference in quality, service, or price. At the finish line, the difference between winners and also-rans is always measured in inches, never in yards.

Look around you: The average organization does a pretty average job. It produces products and provides services that are acceptable, but not outstanding. These organizations pay average wages, earn average rates of return, and operate in environments that, for them, are filled with competitive hazards and risks. Because most organizations are so average, the upstart, the innovator, or the group that hustles or is passionate about doing what it does extremely well is always a threat.

Possibly one-third of the businesses in America are going out of business and their managers don't even know it's happening. One thing managers can do to gain that incremental differential—the competitive edge—is to work on the shirker problem.

When I was a boy in Chicago, my friends and I made a game of trying to get free rides to high school on the Broadway streetcar. We invented all sorts of ruses to get out of paying the 2-cent fare. The reward was not in money saved, but in outfoxing the conductors.

There are also free-riders in most organizations. Free-riders are those who get full benefits but who don't contribute. Shirkers are free-riders. My research in this area has led me to the following thoughts, some of which may be surprising.

1. *Free-riders are behaving rationally.* Why should people give their best effort if they will receive the same reward for lesser efforts? People respond to their perceptions of rewards and efforts. Why would a prudent person consistently do more if the additional effort produced no discernible return? If, for example, your job is to pull on an oar, and the boat has 200 oarsmen, why not fake it? The argument that we are all in the same boat, therefore, pull hard, doesn't motivate the oarsman in this case. Yet, this is a case in which what is rational for one individual creates a negative situation if everyone behaves in the same way.

2. *We are all free-riders.* To some extent, nearly everyone is a free-rider. How many of us are active in our church, PTA, union, or in politics? We ride on the efforts of others.

3. *Free-riders are found in all organizations.* I know of no large organization—with the possible excep-

tion of the United States Army Special Forces—in which there isn't a significant percentage of workers who are shirkers. A study done by John Lewis Partnership, a highly profitable British retail chain in which the employees participate in decision making and in profits, revealed that one-third of their employees admit to working at a marginal level and that they believe they could do much more. If this outstanding firm has so many shirkers, what must be going on in average organizations?

4. *The degree of shirking varies.* There is quite a difference between the factory worker who hides and sleeps four hours on the night shift while his associates do the work and a person who just meets his standard goal. The salesperson who turns in sales reports on calls he never made is different from the one who quits at 3:00 p.m. rather than drive 10 miles to make an extra call. Most shirkers probably aren't free-riders—they're just paying half fare.

Now what can be done about shirkers? Here are some suggestions.

1. *Assign employees to small work teams.* Workers who are in large groups (over fifteen) find it difficult to see the significance of their contributions. Their shirking seems to have no discernible impact on company productivity or profits. "What difference does it make if I don't do my little job perfectly?" they wonder. In small groups, the shirker is under pressure from his peers, and this is more constant and possibly more meaningful than the boss's eagle eye. The small group learns that with

good management it can become a team where everyone's contribution is not only noticed but is considered significant.

2. *Replace competitive systems with a team approach.* The goal is to make everyone a winner. In most competitive systems there are few winners and many losers. Shirkers are losers. How can they be made into winners? Workers need to become an interdependent group. The group may compete against outside groups—other shifts, departments, or companies—but within the group there must be a team. As general manager of the Boston Celtics, Red Auerbach never kept statistics on individual scoring. He was concerned with the big *W,* winning games, which required teamwork.

3. *Have teams participate in setting objectives and standards.* What is management saying to production workers when they are asked to participate in establishing output goals, both in terms of quality and quantity? They're saying, "You are mature, competent adults who are interested in doing a superior job. You want to do this because you are this kind of person and because your team needs you. You also know and have pride in the quality workmanship of your group and the organization as a whole." Managers don't abdicate their responsibilities (they shouldn't do this), but they ask for help and advice on production goals.

4. *Give clear and frequent feedback to the team.* The one thing that motivates everyone is clear and frequent feedback about where you currently are in terms of pre-established goals. For example, ev-

ery employee in the John Lewis department store chain has access to a weekly newspaper that, along with other information, has a complete breakdown of sales for every department in every store in the country. Production workers at Herman Miller in Bath, England, receive a weekly report on their team's output, quality index, and profit contribution.

5. *Require teams to adjust to standards.* Work teams and their leaders are required to meet or surpass the standards they have agreed to. They have both the authority and responsibility for high-level performance. The General Motors truck plant in Shreveport is run on a work team basis. Each team's production is assessed each day, and on the basis of their detailed computer print-outs, they know precisely where and when the problems occurred and who was working on the job at the time.

6. *Ask the team not only to do a job, but to come up with ways to reduce cost and improve the product.* Teams are given more responsibility than individual workers. Since they know more about the jobs they're doing than anyone else, they are asked to come up with cost-reduction and safety improvement ideas. Frequently a specific goal is set, and they're given time—company time—to talk and think about this.

7. *Allow team participation in hiring, training, and evaluating new team members.* One way to build pride is to let employees know that their jobs are difficult and that management values their team ef-

forts. The team may be asked to meet with a potential new team member and to help train this person. The team should have a sense of ownership in both the problems and the success of the company.

8. *Share profits and bonuses.* The results of high performance should be shared through profit-sharing schemes or bonuses. By organizing in small groups or teams, there should be a sense that we—all of us together—have accomplished something significant. "Even though I just assemble the front ends on trucks, I know that I am helping make one of the finest quality vehicles of its type in the world."

Even firms that have developed a team approach and work at it find that they still have problems. Some teams develop group think and are not open to new ideas. Others have poor leadership that may even protect the shirker because he's a good guy. Some shirkers are incorrigible and must be let go.

The suggestions here are not cure-alls. But the alternatives—increasing the number of managers, controllers, and monitors—didn't work for Russia and they don't work in prison factories. In fact, there is some evidence that there's a reverse correlation between increasing management on the shop floor and reduction in quality and productivity.

Horton the elephant listens. He believes that most people are competent and want to contribute, and that those who are shirking don't feel that their contributions are significant. Maybe, like Horton, more of us have to find some way to say, "We need you. The team needs you. Don't let us down."

The Cardini Factor

Have you ever heard of a magician named Cardini? Not Houdini, but Cardini.

Probably not. Yet Cardini devised and presented a unique type of magic act that has never been surpassed. After many false starts, this Welshman who burned with the desire to perform magic, hit upon the idea of playing the role of a London gentleman who had had too much to drink. His act opened with an off-stage voice calling out, "Paging Mr. Cardini! Paging Mr. Cardini!" Then the spotlight picked up a tipsy, monocled Britisher wearing a cape, top hat, and white gloves, and carrying a cane. With unsteady hands, he reached forward and a cigarette materialized between his gloved fingers. He seemed surprised as inexplicable events happened to him. Cards appeared at his fingertips, and when dropped, another group appeared. Through his apparently inebriated eyes, he watched his white silk scarf tie and untie itself—then vanish. It seemed like little demons were playing tricks on him—lighted cigarettes one after another appeared; billiard balls appeared, multiplied, and vanished in his gloved hands. Cardini walked off the stage smoking a huge meerschaum pipe, which materialized from nowhere. There seemed to be no explanation. This was real magic.

I first saw the "Suave Deceiver" in 1946 as a 12-year-old in the Empire Room in Chicago. This was my father's birthday present to me. The music, lighting, and perfect staging set his pantomime act apart. Cardini had one of the highest paid cabaret acts in the world. Presidents Roosevelt and Truman, King George VI, and royalty all over the world invited him to perform. Cardini's act, which was unchanged for 20 years, was only 13 minutes long.

What was it that he did better than anyone else? When I met Cardini at the Chicago Round Table, an informal club for magicians, he gave me some advice. "First you must visualize what you want to be at your very best, and then practice, practice, practice."

Cardini's manipulations weren't complicated. In fact, I could do many of them even as a boy. But he reached a level of brilliance in his art that went beyond what is called sleight of hand. His work was poetry in motion.

By aiming high and focusing on the few things he did exceedingly well, Cardini stood out from all others who have come before or after him.

On a July afternoon in 1964 in Bethany, West Virginia, I stopped to watch a Little League football practice session. A few hundred feet away, the Pittsburgh Steelers were going through their training camp workout on a college football field. What made this coincidence so memorable was that both groups of players were doing exactly the same thing—working on fundamentals.

In his book *Instant Replay*, Jerry Kramer tells how Vince Lombardi intimidated, bullied, and cajoled his first Green Bay Packers team. "He treated everyone alike," notes Kramer. "Like dogs." But, as the story continues, we see how Lombardi inspired his players to give their best efforts. He knew the strengths of each one of them and helped them believe in their own prowess and that of their compatriots. The Packers' high performance required consistently flawless execution of quite basic plays. Each block was absolutely important. The right number of errors was zero. This meant work. This meant practice, practice, and more practice in the basics. Titles, Lombardi believed, are not won by grandstand players, but by teams that are inspired to aim high and to be brilliant in the execution of the basics.

One of the easiest businesses to start is a restaurant. One of the hardest businesses to keep customers happy with over the years is the restaurant business. That is why the turnover rate in this field is so high.

New Orleans is noted for its many fine restaurants. One of the most successful and fascinating is Galatoire's. Here is a restaurant that does no special advertising, and yet, people line up and sometimes wait hours to enter. Galatoire's has never taken reservations and whether you are a homemaker, a CEO, or a movie star, you must wait your turn.

What in the world is going on here? It's not the fancy decor that attracts the customers. Inside, the restaurant looks as though it were caught in a time warp. While this may appeal to some people, it cannot explain the restaurant's magnetic pull.

For over 80 years Galatoire's has followed the same management policies. Like Cardini, they know what they want to do and they practice to perfection the few things they choose to do. Their purpose is unambiguous: They are and have been in the business of preparing and serving extraordinarily fine food and wine without pretension at reasonable prices.

Think about Galatoire's statement of purpose again, and you will see that this tells them exactly what they are not and what they will not do, as well as what they are or should be at their best.

To accomplish this, they follow some hard and fast rules. First, they will prepare fresh food each day. There will never be leftovers. They may run out of something, but yesterday's fish or fowl or torte will not be served today. The chefs (forty-five of them) personally inspect all food themselves. Suppliers must meet their standards—or else. (Just-in-time and zero defect concepts have been operating in this organization before the Japanese ever thought of them.) No frozen fish will be found in these kitchens. The wine stock is small, but of high quality and good value.

Second, waiters play a special role in this organization. Typically they serve no more than three tables and frequently only two. Rather than being assigned to a territory in the restaurant, waiters may be asked for by name, and some of them have served the same customers for 20 years or more. There are no bartenders. Management trusts the waiters. This policy gives the waiters an opportunity to mix the drinks precisely as their customers like them, and there are legendary stories about the phenomenal memories of these preferred waiters and the special services they can provide.

Finally, the same basic dishes, using unchanged recipes, have appeared on the menu for many years. Here's a place that has a unique formula for success—nothing complicated or theatrical. They don't sell the sizzle. Instead, they deliver quality, service, and value.

Doing the right things all the time doesn't happen by accident. Two traits explain Lombardi's and Galatoire's uncommon performance. Both are part of Cardini's dictum— know what it is you are trying to do, and practice, practice, practice. In short, aim high and be brilliant in the basics.

Few managers—whether they run retail stores, manufacturing firms, banks, schools, or hospitals—can actually define what it is that they are trying to do better than anyone else. These managers can't imagine what their enthusiastic customers might say about their organization. They can't visualize or articulate their special *raison d'etre* with clarity. Nor can they spell out the basics that must be rehearsed to perfection.

The Cardini factor is not just good advice for entertainers; it should guide all those who want to succeed.

6

Catalytic Leadership

Most people want to be part of a high-performing team—whether it's a church choir, youth group, debate team, union, or work group. But a group of able and self-confident persons do not automatically make for an outstanding team. Leadership is the agent that, like a catalyst in a chemical reaction, makes something special happen. In organizations the conversion from ordinary to extraordinary happens because people voluntarily choose to give their best to the group's goal. An individual follows the leader not out of fear or because of a bribe, but because the leader lets each member of the team know that only through individual efforts can the team hope to succeed.

Leadership at all levels is critical. But it's important to remember that leadership is not the same as management. You can be a superb administrator—make things run smoothly and meet deadlines within budget constraints—and yet have no leadership ability. On the other hand, you can be a great leader and have only modest administrative skills.

Adding leadership to a group is like adding yeast to dough—something fresh and exciting happens. Leaders don't have to give inspiring speeches or make dramatic demonstrations. Furthermore, the job of catalyst can rotate—people can take turns leading. This is what happens in high-performing organizations.

Leadership can come from a 2-year-old girl who never makes a speech but whose life inspires others or from an 84-year-old man who does make speeches but whose actions are louder than his words. Leadership is the sparkplug that sets off the internal combustion engine of any team. Can leadership be taught? Can it be learned? Read on, and decide for yourself.

Leading by Example

Leaders inspire us to give our best efforts. But a leader doesn't always have to be an extraordinary hero like George Washington, Mahatma Gandhi, Martin Luther King, Jr., or Corazón Aquino. A leader is anyone who demonstrates what we can be at our best, who leads by example.

One of the most inspiring people in my life never made a formal speech, held a high office, or had any special authority or prestige. She's my daughter Jan.

Ever since she was a toddler, Jan had as much energy, enthusiasm, and appetite for life as anyone I've ever known. Born with a sense of fair play and a total lack of fear, she met all obstacles head-on. People of all ages in the little West Virginia village where she grew up knew her and recognized her unique strengths.

Twenty-seven years ago, I went into Jan's room at 5:30 in the morning and found my 2-year-old holding onto the side of her crib, jumping up and down as though the mattress were a trampoline. She greeted me with a huge smile and said, "I'se up [I'm up]." Three days later, she was on an operating table on the sixth floor of a Wheeling hospital. An alert doctor believed Jan had more than a stomach ache. He was right; she had Wilms tumor, a massive encapsulated cancerous growth on one of her kidneys.

My wife Lucy, a close family friend, and I sat in the hospital waiting room for 4½ hours—time does not always fly. Eventually, the surgeon told us he had removed the affected kidney and the tumor, and he had "cleared out" all the spots the tumor had touched. That meant three ribs.

When my wife and I entered the recovery room, there was Jan with tubes sticking in her but still vibrant. "I'se want a hot dog," she said.

Early the next day, the pediatrician confronted me in Jan's room. "Why are you smiling?" he asked.

"Because Jan is doing so well," I replied.

"She is not doing well," he said. "We haven't even started. She needs chemotherapy and weeks of radiation treatment. The probability of recovery is small, and if she does recover, there's an 80 percent chance there will be a recurrence. I want you to face reality. She has to live to be 6 or 7 before you can be sure the cancer will not pop up again."

I suddenly felt the floor drop from under me—I fainted.

When Jan came home from the hospital everyone in the village wanted to show their love and concern for her. They showered her with toys, flowers, love, and affection. But the days ahead were difficult ones. Jan grew pasty white and thin. The radiation treatments were hard on her. She stopped talking to everyone except her big brother Craig. What was going on in her mind?

I grew angry. If there is a God, I thought, I'd choke him. How dare this happen? My stalwart mother-in-law helped bring me back to my senses by saying, "Would you want this terrible thing to happen to any of your other children?"

"No," I answered.

"Out of all of them, which would have the best chance of making it?" she continued.

"Jan," I said.

"And in this village," she continued, "what child has more spunk and spirit than Jan?"

"No one," I answered.

Jan did make it. She made it day by day, week by week. She made herself eat. She tried to keep up with her friends—first on the swing set and later at the skating rink and in the swimming pool. Her strength returned; the scars on her body didn't bother her. The years passed, and by the age of 10 the threat of recurrence was gone.

Today Jan is a strong, bright, beautiful person both inside and out. Through discipline and hard work, she has become a fine swimmer, biker, and runner. She has completed her Ph.D. in microbiology and is now doing research at Dartmouth. She faces life today with the same "I'se up" outlook she had when she was a baby.

She never gave up.

The Elements of Leadership

Leadership and management are not interchangeable concepts. Management—to the extent that this concept refers to skills and knowledge—can be taught. Economic forecasting, capital budgeting, cost accounting, and performance reviews can be learned in the classroom and applied to the organization.

But management is not leadership. In fact, no matter how rigorous and academically powerful in their application, the management courses that are taught at most universities are neither the necessary nor the sufficient cause of success. A little reflection should make this point clear.

Alexander the Great accomplished his noteworthy achievements without computers or accounting systems. Abraham Lincoln, a school dropout, knew nothing of the formal management concepts we teach. How many of the trustees at Stanford University, most of whom are successful businessmen, would have high scores on the General Management Aptitude Test?

To be successful, one doesn't have to be a charismatic leader like Gandhi, Churchill, or JFK. Ordinary people, such as high-school principals, production managers, ministers, drama coaches, and gas-station operators can get extraordinary results from other people. This extraordinary performance happens because of leadership. Although successful leaders share no common heritage or education, they share some common qualities.

Vision. Those who lead others to above-average performance do it because they have the capacity to visualize how the organization might be at its best. Not only do they "see it" more clearly than the rest of us, they also articulate their vision. They are excited by their "dream," and a glimpse of their vision inspires us. We want to be part of something special—not ordinary—and here is our chance. We are energized, and we voluntarily choose to help transform a vision into reality.

Visionary managers are not problem solvers. They are creative problem finders. W.T. Grant's, the largest variety store in America in the 1960s, went belly up in the 1970s, not because of its inability to apply modern management concepts, but because the company lost its way. Grant's was selling the wrong merchandise at the wrong locations. No computer system could save it. Wal-Mart, a small firm in 1960, has grown into one of the largest retailers in the world because of the vision of one man—Sam Walton.

Visionary managers also see strengths in the rest of us that others miss. They are not soft-headed romantics, but they tend to grow and enable others to grow, according to their vision. Ordinary managers expect less, and that is what they get.

Passionate persistence. Leaders not only have a more lucid vision of what can be, they also have a passionate commitment to their vision. They ignore the naysayers and those who want more analyses and studies. They don't think of themselves as risk takers. They know they are on the right path, and they won't give in, give up, or back off. They are dogged, and when we ordinary people are intimidated or tired, they refuse to let us quit. They stand out because they are rooted by their convictions and vision.

Moral courage. Leaders are not only committed to their dream of what the project or department can be and determined to get on with it, but they also are committed to each member of the team. They are not "stars" but player-coaches. George Washington did, in fact, feed his men before he ate. His soldiers often were unpaid and poorly clothed, but they were highly motivated. Brandon Beach, a restaurant manager in Shreveport, will fill in for any job, no matter how dirty or hard, when he is needed.

Moral courage is what it takes to admit you are fallible and that you need the help of others. Moral courage is also what it takes to go against the prevailing group if you believe that it is in the best long-term interest of the organization to do so. Moral courage is a rare quality.

Integrity. There is nothing slick or political about this quality. Integrity is what lets the members of a group accept the leader's decisions and behavior because they believe he or she is a fair person who does what's right and not what's expedient. Even if they disagree with the call, they can accept it.

Does this mean that management courses are of no value? Absolutely not. Johnny Weissmuller's swimming records stood longer than any modern swimmer's have. Yet today 14-year-old girls can beat his time. Weight training, flip turns, and coaching do matter. Better technical skills are needed to be competitive in both sports and management. Alexander the Great would need modern technology in today's world.

But the vital difference in outstanding performance in almost all areas of human endeavor is leadership. And leadership requires skills, values, and ways of thinking and behaving that rarely are taught in the classrooms of even our best universities.

Where, then, does one learn vision, moral courage, passionate persistence, and integrity? Is there a Wizard of Oz who will dispense it? Of course not! Need you be born with these qualities? No!

Leadership skills and values are learned but not taught. They are learned best while we are growing and developing. They are learned on playing fields and debate teams, in sorority houses and church groups. They are learned in the home and in groups and small communities where each individual believes he or she can make a difference. One reason why great leaders often emerge from small towns and small colleges is because these places provide both the proper environment and incentive system for leadership development.

Management is needed for efficiency. Leadership is needed for extraordinary performance.

Don't Blame the Messenger

Visiting the dentist is supposed to be a dreadful experience. Not so for me on one particular Thursday.

As I left the dentist's office, I thought to myself, "What a thoroughly professional exchange we had." The dentist explained that he wanted to help me keep my teeth and a good healthy bite. But to do this, he needed time to study my mouth and then plan the options with me. He could start by drilling and capping, but in the long run, a total approach was preferable.

This informative visit made me wonder about how some other business is transacted. Consider the following events.

> *Event 1.* A travel agent working for a highly esteemed agency was too busy to return a call made by one of my associates. A day later, when he requested information on an inexpensive flight to Washington, D.C., he was given a price quote. A phone call to another agency came up with a fare that was $70 cheaper. Everyone makes a mistake, but....

Event 2. My family and I purchased a wrought-iron patio set from a respected furniture store. Our salesperson made nearly every error possible. We weren't greeted or acknowledged as individuals; we weren't asked about our needs or preferences; and the clerk demonstrated little product knowledge, didn't understand the warranty provisions, and didn't affirm our purchase decision. To add to her unprofessionalism, she chewed gum—loudly.

Event 3. One day I went to a local restaurant that's famous for its lunch menu and decor. The waitress greeted my party with indifference. When I asked about the specialty of the day, we were told it wasn't very good. The chowder I ordered came after a 20-minute wait, and the sandwiches we'd asked for appeared at different times. We never got a refill on coffee because the waitress was busy chatting with a coworker.

A few days before this last event I was reading an article about a study of air conditioners in the *Harvard Business Review*. According to the author, the very best American-made products would not meet the minimum acceptable standards in Japan. Both quality of workmanship and dependability were substandard. But the sad fact is that a vast array of products and services that are just marginally acceptable—not just air conditioners, cameras, and cars—are being offered in the marketplace.

There is a well-known story about a king who would reward the messenger who brought him good news and behead the messenger who brought a bleak message. Why should I be upset with a travel agent, a furniture salesperson, or a waitress who appears to lack competence or civility? Aren't they but messengers? What is the message they are delivering? Isn't it clear? The management is not doing its job.

These workers are like most of us—quite decent and ordinary people. Their performance is poor most likely because they lack the tools they need (computer technology for the travel agency), proper training, motivation, and management support to do their jobs.

Managers may want to deny this assertion or skirt the issue, but low-level performance from employees generally means low-level management. Shoddy products come from shoddy managers. Rude or indolent clerks probably mean rude, indolent, or indifferent managers.

Some of us in education like to take personal credit for the high performance of our superior students. We often look on low performance as a problem inherent in the student and not our fault. However, a few master teachers will produce above-average performance from poor to average students. Like good managers who have high and clear expectations, these teachers create an environment in which students want to excel. They won't accept poor work. They coach students and give them feedback and reward good performance.

Fortunately there are many managers who are on the road to being master managers. These managers know the vast capacity that average persons—most of us—have to contribute. They also know the power of the three R's—responsibility, recognition, and reward—to motivate men and women to be consistently high performers. The philosophy and strategies of these superior managers are translated into high-quality products and services, and their message is carried all the way down the line to the customer.

My dentist is obviously close to the customer, and the message he delivered to me was that he wants a long-term relationship that will best serve my needs. Excellent organizations around the world follow the same concepts as my dentist.

What message are your employees delivering? What message are you sending?

Why Don't They Do What I Tell Them to Do?

Why don't your employees do what you tell them to do? Don't you tell them to be good to customers, polite to visitors, careful in shipping goods, forceful in selling, and patient with subordinates? Why is it that your good intentions are not carried out?

It could be that you didn't communicate your idea properly. If someone told you to cook a wonderful meal and set the table beautifully, you might pause and wonder what exactly is a wonderful meal and how does a beautiful table look. You need a specific recipe and specific instructions.

When we tell the receptionist to be polite or a bank teller to be patient or a salesperson to be assertive or a factory worker to be careful, what have we really said?

What all of us must do if we want higher performance is to be much better teachers and coaches. Whether they're workers, students, or toddlers, people need specific instructions on how to deal with specific incidences. They need hands-on simulations and peer feedback. They need step-by-step guidelines for everyday procedures—whether packing materials, sorting inventory, taking phone messages, dealing with irate customers, giving performance reviews, operating machines, writing a term paper, or picking up toys.

A *Fortune* magazine article once described how three successful firms teach people how to sell. What they have in common are specific steps for different situations, and hours of practice with peer group feedback. Training is time consuming and hard work. But although it's extremely important, it isn't urgent. Is it any wonder, then, that most of us put it off or do it in a slapdash way?

The next time you visit a McDonald's, observe how all the order clerks behave. Every step from the initial eye contact to the final thank-you has been programmed. If done according to plan, it should be the same in all restaurants in all states. Spontaneity is lost, but a high level of quality in customer relations is gained.

All management-level employees at Ball Jar Corporation in Muncie, Indiana, have the same product information, which they present in the same sequence and with the same emphasis. And this presentation is impressive to prospective customers because they hear the same story from everyone in the organization.

Watch a commercial airline pilot go through his or her pre-established route before takeoff or a surgeon scrub for an operation or a mechanic service an expensive earth-moving machine, and you'll notice how quality, reliability, and consistency are built into their procedures.

The next time you have an exchange with a bank teller, find a defective product, buy an airplane ticket, or have a telephone conversation with a secretary, see if you think there isn't a lot of slippage between management's intention and your particular case.

You don't have to be a giant to stand out in a field of average persons. This is the substance of the +10 Percent Principle. In fact, standouts need only be slightly taller. Organizations that stand out are not dramatically different from average organizations. The people, equipment, and techniques are largely interchangeable. But high-achieving organizations have managers who are willing to invest the hard work, patience, and funds it takes to provide professional skills to every worker.

The next time you hear a manager talk about the stupid and infuriating thing her employee did, or a teacher tell you how poorly his students did on an exam, you may want to think about the primary reason people don't do what they're told to do.

Productive Procrastination

Nine years ago my children bought me a French 10-speed touring bicycle. It wasn't until the winter snow melted away that I had a chance to try it out. The first ride ended up being the last ride.

A woman, apparently preoccupied, took a sharp left turn in her car, accelerated, and crashed head-on into me on my new bike. The impact of the collision sent me flying through her windshield. I rolled off the hood of the car and fell to the pavement. My neck was broken, my face and body lacerated, and my left hip fractured.

The next morning my doctor asked me to sign a release for an operation he was going to perform on my hip. I told him I had little pain and that I could move. In fact, using a walker I had shuffled to the bathroom early that morning. This statement surprised him and he warned me not to do it again. After looking at the x-rays, he told me that I could consider conservative treatment—stay on crutches for several weeks and hope the bones healed themselves. They did!

You know the old adage "Don't put off until tomorrow what you can do today." This generally is good advice, but there are some important exceptions. Mine was one of those cases.

One thing all managers have in common is that they are responsible for making decisions. The athletic coach, symphony conductor, school principal, hospital adminstrator, shop foreman, and corporate executive are all decision makers. Clearly some decisions need to be made quickly. But it is surprising how many important decisions that have no particular urgency are made quickly—sometimes too quickly. Some decisions can and should be put off as long as they can be. A friend of mine used to call this idea productive procrastination.

There is a parable in which Jesus came upon a woman about to be stoned to death for committing adultery. Jesus didn't use any supernatural power to save the woman in this story. He simply drew away from the crowd, knelt down, and began to scrawl in the sand. What was going on?

This is a good example of productive procrastination. To see why, think of some of the ways others might have handled this situation.

What if James Bond had come on this scene? Can you imagine his helicopter hovering overhead as he drops down on a rope and whisks the beautiful woman away? Not bad!

Or what if Clint Eastwood had appeared? Can't you just see him, gun in hand, telling the crowd to "Go ahead, make my day."

F. Lee Bailey would have still another approach. He would tell the crowd what the legal implications of their actions would be or he possibly would defend the woman on the grounds of mistaken identity or insufficient evidence.

Jesus might have been thinking about His options as He scrawled in the sand. Finally he came up with an elegant solution, one that required no getaway tactics, coercion, or fast talking: "...He that is without sin among you, let him first cast a stone at her." What a brilliant solution.

Rather than making the decision quickly, Jesus used the principle of productive procrastination. By slowing down the decision-making process, He was not bound to take action on the basis of His first reaction.

Managers frequently have a hard time separating urgent decisions from important ones. Some urgent decisions are also important. But it's surprising how many urgent decisions are really of low priority.

Conversely, many important decisions carry no sense of urgency. We may be better off taking the maximum allowable time for these important decisions.

Let's assume that you're considering three people for a promotion to an important post. This decision can be made quickly. But it need not be. General Dwight D. Eisenhower was noted for surrounding himself with first-rate people. He thought these appointments were among the most important decisions he made, and he wouldn't be pressed into a hasty one. As with a long engagement, there are times when taking the extra time costs little. When a time-out is called in basketball, good coaches use it.

Years ago my sales manager, William Hoelke, was faced with a decision. The product that he had introduced to America, Marshmallow Creme, was doing poorly. People didn't know how to use this sticky, gooey substance, and its shelf life was limited. Top management asked him to either drop the product from our retail line or to find a way to dramatically improve it. They wanted results.

I advised him to drop the product immediately. Even though it had a large gross margin, I thought it was a dumb product and found it hard to be sincere and enthusiastic in pitching it. I made a strong case for how our time could be better spent on other activities.

Bill listened to me, but he didn't take my advice. Rather, he asked management for one month to work on the problem. Four weeks later, he presented a new promotional program to our sales team and the executive committee. What an unusual presentation it was! There, on the boardroom table, were several plates of fudge. No file cards or handouts; just fudge. He wanted everyone to try it. We liked it. In fact, we liked it a lot. It was creamy and had a familiar chocolate flavor.

Then Bill put a bag of Hershey's chocolate chips and a big jar of Pennant Brand Marshmallow Creme with a new label on the boardroom table. He held up a rather crude ad, which showed how easy it was to combine these two ingredients to make delicious fudge.

Bill Hoelke had observed that our bottled marshmallow cream was selling in rural New England communities. Further investigation revealed that New Englanders discovered that this product, which eliminated the need to melt down regular marshmallows in a double boiler, made a good fudge. Marshmallow fudge was an old standby in New Hampshire, but hardly known in Indiana or Colorado. No one in our laboratory or advertising office thought that the product could be used this way. They believed it was only good for topping ice cream or cake.

That year Hoelke organized a national advertising campaign around his concept. Little Pennant Marshmallow Creme of Columbus, Indiana, teamed up with the giant Hershey Company of Hershey, Pennsylvania. The campaign not only won critical acclaim from the advertising community for its cleverness, it convinced millions of people to try to make marshmallow fudge.

If Bill Hoelke had listened to a young Barrie Richardson, he would have earned my respect for being a decisive and quick-acting manager; the world would probably never have had marshmallow fudge in such abundance; and I wouldn't have been taught the relevance of the principle of productive procrastination.

No doubt, you can think of other uses for this simple but powerful idea.

They Really Blew That One, Didn't They?

Flight 881 left Tampa on time. About 30 minutes into the flight, the plane's captain told the passengers that his instruments showed that the landing gear might be defective. In a rich, confident voice, he told us that we were flying lower and slower than our flight plan called for, and that the ground crew in Memphis was alerted to our potential problem. He assured us that everything was under control, and that he would give us additional instructions as we approached the airport.

I wasn't particularly concerned, since this had happened to me once before in Europe and things had worked out quite well. However, many of the passengers were panicky.

As we neared the Memphis airport, the captain's deep, friendly voice came over the speaker system. "Please remove all pointed objects from your pockets. Our attendant will be by to collect them. We will be landing on a runway set aside for us. You will notice several emergency vehicles on the field. In my opinion, we will not need them. If there is an explosion, emergency doors will open. The cabin attendants will also show you how to brace yourselves and how to place your head on your crossed arms. They will tell you when to assume this position, which you will hold until I signal that all is well."

People were now quite anxious. The woman next to me had her rosary beads out, and there were tears in her eyes as she recited the names of her four children over and over again.

"Assume the position, assume the position," a flight attendant screamed in a shrill voice.

The plane came down gently, and the wheels hit ground with only a small jolt—the landing gear had worked perfectly.

After everyone sighed, the captain's voice came on again. "Thank you for being such good troopers. This is an experience none of us will forget. Thank you for your help." We all burst into applause.

He continued, "Many of you have missed your connections and some of you have other problems. There will be a person at the gate waiting to help you." Again, many of us applauded.

As we left the plane, we shook hands with the crew; some people hugged the flight attendants. We felt good about being safe, and we felt that the pilot and crew had been extremely professional in the way they had shared information and prepared us for landing. They could not have done a better job.

When we got off the plane we looked around for someone to help us sort out our flight plans. *No one was there!*

Carrying a suitcase, a woman in her seventies said to an employee at a boarding counter, "I was on the plane that made an emergency landing. How do I get to my next plane?"

The person at the counter responded sharply, "I don't know about any emergency landing. You'll have to wait in line or go over to the main terminal."

A young business executive standing next to me looked me in the eye and said disgustedly, "They really blew that one, didn't they?"

And they had. In this instance, defeat had been pulled from the jaws of victory.

What went wrong? Was the airline understaffed? Did the message not get through? Did the pilot just assume the managers on the ground would take care of his passengers? Who knows? Customers don't care about the cause of a snafu. All they want is efficient, courteous service during each step of the trip. Sounds simple. And it is—but it isn't easy.

Dr. Robert Brewer, one of the most highly respected management trainers in America, calls each one of these steps "the moment of truth." Brewer believes that many employees may have 50 to 100 moments of truth each day.

Don't most of us have a clear picture of what we expect from a good hotel? I once attended a weekend convention at a Fort Worth hotel. My room was nicer than I had anticipated. The service in the dining room was excellent, and the food was pretty good too. I thought they were doing a good job. Then it came time to check out. Apparently one computer was down, and several people were challenging their bills. It took 44 minutes to check out of the hotel. What went wrong? Who knows? But I know that there were three people in the manager's office doing something—who knows what—rather than pitching in to help us check out.

Each link in the chain must work perfectly to make a customer feel good about service. The Fort Worth hotel did ninety-nine things right, but they blew it in the end.

What customers expect and want is really quite simple. But it's very difficult to meet these expectations. I like the concept of "contact points" rather than the more dramatic "moment of truth." A contact point is needed to get the gasoline engine to spark. An eight-cylinder car can run on seven plugs, but not smoothly. All contact points in the system need to work properly.

Last spring, a major U.S. retailer sent out a beautiful catalog featuring its summer collection. The models, merchandise, photography, paper, and printing all sent the same message—quality.

One of my friends ordered three items at the beginning of May. In June she got a computer-generated letter asking her to be patient since the demand for the items she'd ordered was so great. At the end of June she received one item in the mail along with another computer-generated letter telling her that the other goods were coming. Toward the end of July she got a refund check.

Think about this. The summer season was coming to an end and her May order was not filled. The store's merchandising and advertising people probably felt great about their catalog since they had to turn customers away. The bottom line looked very good.

But what about the thousands of potential customers whose expectations were not met? What about the moments of truth, the contact points? How many people have bad feelings about this firm? How will they respond to the next catalog? What might the store have done to make up for their disappointment? Could it have converted these upset people into committed and joyful patrons? Simple, but not easy.

This failure to meet expectations isn't only found in business. Recently a president of a manufacturing firm told me how bad he felt about a well-known college in New England. Three of his children had gone to this college. When his youngest daughter was set to graduate, the family requested six tickets to the graduation ceremony— five for the family and one for an 88-year-old grandmother. But five was the maximum number the college would give. That was the rule; no exceptions. One of the family would not be able to attend. The family decided that none of them—including the young woman who was to graduate—would go. Think about it. Wouldn't you put an 88-year-old woman on stage, if need be, to show appreciation for a family that had sent three of its children to the college? They really blew that one, didn't they?

Management is not complicated. Yet, getting people to be persistent and passionate about trying to arrange transactions in a way that benefits the customer and still profits the firm is a challenge.

Whoever said managing for excellence was easy? Exhilarating and mind-stretching yes, but not easy.

Why Should Anyone Give Their Best?

A few minutes after I had completed a workshop on how outstanding organizations get extraordinary performance from ordinary people, a man came up to me and said, "You have to come by my factory and help me get my employees committed to the company."

"Why should your workers be committed to your organization?" I asked. The fellow gave me a funny look and walked away.

Like many managers, this well-intentioned man had the whole idea of employee commitment turned upside down.

One mark of an outstanding business—whether it be a multinational company or your local shoe-repair shop—is a basic commitment on the part of nearly all employees to give their best to the firm. But this isn't the normal state of affairs. In fact, even when it's clear to an employee that a particular company policy is in the best interest of the firm and is also in the best interest of all employees, many people still deliberately choose to behave in a way that hurts the organization.

Why don't employees always behave in a way that will benefit the firm? Isn't everyone in the same boat together?

Aristotle believed that if a person knew what was best for the state, he would behave in a constructive way. Aristotle might assert that poor behavior by employees—sloppy work, tardiness, pilfering—represents shortsightedness in employees' mental calculations. But Aristotle would be wrong!

Even if you know your efforts will help the common good, and that you will share in the common results, you aren't motivated by reason alone to commit your best effort. Of course, if everyone loafs on the job, output will fall, costs will rise, and profits will be diminished.

The traditional and most frequently used method of keeping workers from shirking is the boss—the taskmaster. By standing over the worker, he or she can detect any malingering and punish the shirker.

Clearly this approach can work. The pyramids were built by slaves who were supervised by a taskmaster, and the pyramids are still standing—as is this system of management. But this system is far from perfect. First, the taskmaster is not working. It now takes one person to oversee ten others. Second, under this system workers will work only when they are being watched, and since these persons are considered to be mere labor-power machines—like donkeys—they will not commit their intellectual and creative capacities to their tasks.

What a wasteful process. Contemporary workers are not slaves and there are no longer whips in the workplace, but anyone who has ever worked in a highly regimented and autocratic organization knows how demotivating this environment can be.

Whenever you find workers voluntarily giving their best to the organization you generally will find that management has earned the trust and respect of the employees. In addition to setting high standards, which most employees want, managers demonstrate their commitment to the workers by

1. *Respecting the dignity and worth of every person.* This cannot be a phony show. Managers can-

not learn this attitude in a university course. Either managers actually believe and act as though each employee has creative ideas to contribute and is a person who can be trusted, or they do not.

2. *Asking for suggestions.* Why should management have all the fun? Seeing one's ideas put into practice is a motivating experience for everyone. How do you feel when someone listens to you?

3. *Providing long-term employment arrangements.* If employees know they are dispensable or easily replaced—like an interchangeable part—they have no motivation to give their best. Managers need to be committed to giving security of employment.

4. *Providing professional development opportunities.* The job is a place where all employees can continue to grow in competence and confidence. Managers need to be committed to the long-term growth of all workers who want to advance. After all, this firm is "their firm." They are vital team members—not mules or machines.

5. *Providing quality work areas.* One way management demonstrates how much they respect their employees is by the kind of working spaces they provide. The telephone plant in my home town is an example of what a world-class factory can look like. The concrete floors are spotless, the noise is minimal, and the air smells fresh. Designer furnishings aren't necessary, but employees deserve good tools and neat, clean work environments. They should be proud to show their families and friends where they work.

6. *Providing a profit-sharing system.* The goal of every company should be to motivate everyone on staff to think and act as though they were owners of the firm. This means that everyone would be concerned with customer satisfaction, quality, productivity, and cost reduction. Instead of simply mouthing the cliche, "We're all in the same boat," managers need to demonstrate that fact by linking the company's performance to individual and group bonuses. This is not a new idea, but one that many high-performing organizations, both large and small, practice.

Why should employees feel committed to give their best to their organization? Here is how Nobel Feldman, president of Harrison Company, Inc., one of the fastest growing food wholesalers in America, answered this question:

> My employees are committed to this company because they know we are committed to providing superior customer service and they know we need quality people like themselves to fill these demanding jobs. We are committed to be above reproach in all our dealings with suppliers, customers, and with persons in the community. Employees are proud of our way of doing business. And, of course, they know we are committed to them.

Why should your employees be committed to you or your organization?

Never Give Up

Wesley Attaway, an entrepreneur and investment banker, concluded a Friday night seminar with twelve mature

MBA candidates by noting, "You must ask yourself what it is that is motivating you. What is it that you really value in life? Money is a score card. However, it is not an end in itself. How do you want to live your life?"

His provocative remarks jolted me into thinking about what my mentor and friend, Perry Epler Gresham, pointed out in his book, *With Wings as Eagles*. How we live our lives depends, to a large degree, on the metaphor we choose to describe our life and reasons for living.

If we see ourselves as machines, we can talk about replacement parts and getting tune-ups. We see mileage accumulate on our bodies and we wear down and ultimately end up in a junkyard. Or, we might select the metaphor of a tree. In this case, we see ourselves as part of nature going through a life cycle of youth, maturity, and inevitable decline. We eventually fall and rot away.

Perry Gresham believes that although there is some truth in these metaphors of the life process, they ignore a basic fact of human nature. We are more than machines and different than other living things. We have the capacity to renew. Sure, our hair grays and we lose some physical strength, but he maintains that every decade brings a renewal of energy and vitality, and we can find new sources of joy and deep fulfillment as we mature. Envy of others shrinks us; there is so much in this world for everyone that we can and should be thrilled for others when good things happen to them. There is no need to rust or rot. We, like the eagle in Isaiah, can be renewed and rise up and ascend to new heights.

Is this a lot of sentimental rubbish? Is Gresham preaching some form of self-deception?

I believe Gresham is articulating a powerful truth. I believe his message not because of statistical studies, but because I have found this happening to me every decade. And persons who seem vital at 70, 80, and even 90 years of age have told me of how waves of new energy flow into their lives in a continuing cycle.

There is another reason why I believe Gresham's theory. Perry Gresham happens to be my hero.

Everyone at all ages and through all stages of life needs a hero. Heroes can't be gods. Heroes can't be comic-strip characters like Superman or Rambo, or literary characters like John Galt or Odysseus. For me heroes must be men and women who breathe and bleed.

Gresham's life seems larger than life. How could one person do so much in 84 years? He was a successful road builder and rancher at 19, first in his class at Texas Christian University, professor of Greek and philosophy, church leader, humorist, serious scholar, lecturer with an international reputation, college president, businessman, bibliophile, and dedicated golfer.

Milton Friedman told me Perry Epler Gresham was the most fascinating man he ever met. John F. Kennedy, Richard Nixon, and Lyndon Johnson all happily accepted honorary degrees from him. Honors from citizens' groups, universities, foundations, and government were given him throughout his career. Pearl Buck, Archibald MacLeish, Mark van Doren, and many other literary figures were his friends. But it is not because he accomplished so much that I chose him for a hero. Nor is it because so many talented people respect him.

No, Perry Gresham is my hero for one reason—his spirit. Some people write about the uniqueness of the human spirit, but only a few can act out the script. Perry Gresham does both.

A few years ago, Perry was scheduled to visit Centenary College, and I looked forward to seeing him lift the vision and self-worth of all who came in contact with him. There is absolutely no one I have met who can instruct and inspire listeners and delight an audience as well as he.

However, when I called his office to confirm his travel arrangements, his secretary told me that he had had emergency prostate surgery, and that I could talk with him in the hospital in Wheeling, West Virginia.

Twelve hours after the procedure he was charming and vibrant. He told me of his plans for the future and how he would spend his life. He made me laugh over one of his terrible puns and promised to come to Centenary in the spring. Before I hung up, I asked him to write out what he told me on the phone. I needed his wisdom, and so do others.

October 31, 1986

Dear and cherished friend:

On this late October morning I have a whole new outlook on life. The medical experts have found a somewhat developed malignancy in my old body. They promise to keep me alive just as long as possible. My question is what do I do now?

My will to live is undiminished; it may even be stronger and more determined than ever. I have no inclination of yielding to despair. While my strength holds out, I shall fight for life. Whether it be for a day, a year, a decade, or a score of years, I shall emphasize the quality of life and find joy and meaning in every day. Methuselah, with all of his 969 years of spare time, could do no more.

This traumatic experience has brought with it a renewal of challenge, opportunity and zest for life.

These shortened days demand a careful review of my priorities. Since I have no time to waste, I shall think, write and speak with enough courage and cheer to share with my friends who, like me, run into obstacles and dangers along the way. As the days go by you will hear from me about new ideas and insights that are now mine.

As I look out across the beautiful Ohio River from Ohio Valley Medical Center, I am thinking about my friends. Before long, [my wife] Aleece will be down here to keep me company. I am free from any self-pity and keen on my next visit with you.

Thank God for these seven decades, and thank God for the next one. You are my friend, and I send every good wish.

Sincerely,
Perry E. Gresham

What do you think of my hero? Does he have the moral courage, determination, and unshakeable faith you want in your hero?

How do contemporary heroes square off against mine?

How would you answer Wes Attaway's question: What is it that you really value in life?

Everyone a Teacher!

I don't believe everything in life is relative—at least not in terms of human activities and conduct. Some books are better than others; some French breads look, smell, and taste better than others; and some professions do make more of a difference in this world than others.

Teaching, preaching, and healing are at the top of my list. But, without a doubt, teaching comes first. Maybe because a truly good teacher can make as much as or more of an impact on the lives of others as a minister or a medical worker. Maybe I believe this because a gifted teacher is, in many ways, a rabbi, a minister, a priest, a healer, a guide, a leader, a servant, and an enabler. Maybe I believe this because I know that what teachers do when they are in good form is what parents and politicians and principals should do.

What are the characteristics of a great teacher, and how can their qualities and behavior be used by leaders in other areas?

Competence

The first requisite of a teacher is competence. This may sound simple-minded and self-evident, but it is neither.

Have you ever known a teacher who was marginally qualified? Have you ever been instructed by a person whose knowledge was defunct? Have you ever had a person who was neither competent nor confident try to teach you cribbage, tennis, or bread-baking?

Competence is a never-ending quest. Great teachers know that teaching and learning are interactive processes that take place in their own minds. First and foremost, teachers must have a command of facts, algorithms, principles, and ways of thinking that they know are powerful and useful. A teacher must have something to teach.

How often do we find symptoms of incompetence in our daily lives? Have you ever come across a hotel desk clerk who is poorly trained and is as enthusiastic as a zombie? Or how about an attorney who, rather than saying "I don't know," fakes it and gives an answer with feigned confidence that may be wrong? How many meetings have you attended that were poorly planned, organized, and led? How many times have you taken your car in for repairs and had to return it to the garage because it still didn't work properly?

We have every right to expect competence in those who are paid to serve us, and we also should expect our bosses and leaders to be competent. Competence is a moving goal. Good teachers are in a never-ending quest for increased competence.

Contagious Enthusiasm for What They Are Teaching

While competence is a necessary condition for a good teacher, it alone is not sufficient. We have all had teachers who were knowledgeable, but who were as interesting as dishwater. They exhibit no love of their topic and their lack of vitality is passed on to their students. On the other hand, some of us have had teachers whose immense enthusiasm for their discipline so sparked our curiosity that we came to discover that topics such as microeconomics and medieval history were fascinating.

Recently I talked to a man who was cleaning a men's room at the Dallas airport. "This place is really spotless. You do a great job," I remarked to the custodian.

"Thank you," he said. "I am only required to do this three times a shift, but I do it five times."

"This place is cleaner than my bathroom at home," I said.

He beamed at me and replied, "It's cleaner than everyone's bathroom at home. I am a professional."

He looked me straight in the eye. There was no arrogance in his demeanor, but rather, he exuded a pride that comes from high performance. He did a common job uncommonly well, and he was eager to tell me about it.

Contrast this with the behavior of a salesclerk in a menswear department who reluctantly waited on me one rainy Saturday morning. My asking him for help had interrupted the conversation he was having with another salesperson, and my very presence obviously irritated him. He may have known a great deal about button-down oxford cloth shirts, but he didn't communicate much enthusiasm or friendliness. I had gone into the store intending to buy six shirts. I left empty-handed.

How many people are there at all levels in all organizations who, though competent, display no passion for what they're doing? Competence attracts, but enthusiasm ignites.

Belief in the Inherent Dignity and Immense Capacity of Every Student

Outstanding teachers have something to teach and are excited about their topic. They also believe that every single student can learn the skills and concepts they are teaching. They know that some students take more time than others do or may need to learn the material in a different way. Great teachers are patient coaches. Everyone can learn to swim, play the piano, and do algebra problems. Not everyone will be a high performer in all those areas, but everyone can meet high minimum standards. It may take longer, but almost any goal can be reached if the student chooses to give his or her best.

The movie *Stand and Deliver* is an example of an actual situation that's more dramatic than any fictional tale could ever be. Who could ever believe that one person, a single teacher named Jaime Escalante, could motivate a class of underprivileged high-school students whom others believed were slow learners to pass the College Advanced Placement Mathematics Examination? And his achievement was not a one-shot fluke. Year after year, more of his students passed this demanding exam than did all the students in the state of Louisiana.

Escalante didn't use high-tech equipment. He used a blackboard, chalk, and his remarkable gift of coaching. He uncovered in his students wellsprings of talent that they did not know they had. He expected high performance and would not accept less. He was not an adversary, but a guide, a mentor, and a friend who affirmed, prodded, pushed, and pulled students to breathtaking intellectual heights. And by using mathematics to show his students how powerful their minds were, he boosted their sense of self-worth and self-confidence.

Leaders and managers also need to see every person as being endowed with untapped intellectual and creative capacities. Managers must remind themselves that a promotion in rank or to a higher level of authority doesn't make that person more intelligent, sensitive, or imaginative. A person's brain doesn't grow in capacity with a new job title. Every worker, like every student, can be a high-performing problem-finder and problem-solver.

Willingness to Serve as a Model of a Developing Person

Good teachers listen. Good teachers try to learn from their students. Good teachers are open to competitive ideas, invite constructive conflict, encourage debate, welcome those who challenge hidden assumptions, and question facts. Good teachers aren't afraid to reveal their own imperfections and insecurities. They aren't gods, but fallible mortals, struggling human beings who, like their students, are trying to grow into compassionate, rational, healthy, productive persons. They serve as real-life models—not fictionalized heroes—of what it means to try to live a life full of discovery, joy, and meaningful work.

What would be going on in our department stores, factories, schools, government agencies, banks, hospitals, and churches if everyone who had any responsibility emulated the great teacher model?

What would family life be like if parents followed these concepts? How would your own life change if you hyphenated your title? I'm a salesperson-teacher; I'm a nurse-teacher; I'm a carpenter-teacher; I'm a banker-teacher; I'm a mother-teacher; I'm a student-teacher.

What would an organization look like and how might it perform if every single person had a high level of demonstrable competence, a contagious passion for his or her job, and an authentic belief in the dignity, ability, and capacity of everyone, including themselves, and attempted to lead his or her life as a model of a good person in the making?

To be catalytic leaders we need not change the people around us—only ourselves. Why don't you and I become good teachers?

7

The +10 Percent
Principle in Action

We have seen that outstanding organizations—whatever their unique mission—are both well-managed and well-led. Their managers create an environment in which ordinary people are invited to participate in the continuous improvement of their teams' activities. Leaders in these organizations have found ways to release the productive energies of ordinary people and to stimulate them to give their best.

High-performing organizations have certain characteristics in common. All of them emphasize not only high levels of performance, but also high levels of worker satisfaction. These two characteristics seem to feed on each other—high performance generates high levels of satisfaction, which, in turn, generate high performance. Leaders of these organizations have a clear vision, high expectations, and long-term commitments to their employees. They have found ways to measure individual and group performance and they link rewards to contributions. Most people in these organizations have a sense of common purpose, and they believe that their particular organization has high ethical values.

In this chapter we'll examine a formula for excellence and take a close look at five case studies in excellence that illustrate many of the points made in this and the preceding sections.

- Unlike many public utilities, which behave like sleeping monopolies, Tampa Electric Company is a model of alertness. Much of the company's success is due to its employees, who actively develop the leadership potential of their coworkers. The "Tampa Triangle" concepts used at this firm can work anywhere.

- John Lewis Partnership is not well-known in the United States. Yet, this British company, which operates a chain of department stores and supermarkets, has millions of loyal customers and thousands of highly motivated employees. One of the most fascinating organizations I have ever studied, it is organized and managed unlike any firm I know.

- Chaparral Steel is possibly the most productive specialty steel company in the world. While many U.S. steel firms have either floundered or gone out of business, Chaparral has flourished. How does it manage to get such extraordinary performance?

- Alcoholics Anonymous has been called the least organized organization in the world. Yet, it is also one of the most successful organizations and offers important lessons for all organizations and leaders everywhere.

- Public school administrators have found it increasingly difficult to improve student performance. And the performance of underprivileged minority students in city schools—even after years of busing and curriculum experiments—continues to lag far behind the national average. Yet, there are over fifty public schools across the country that have adopted a unique "management model" for energizing teachers, parents, and staff to work together to boost student performance. The results to date have been astonishing.

These outstanding organizations have learned how to make the +10 Percent Principle work for them.

A Formula for Excellence

Isn't it funny how one's attitudes and opinions change over the years? Thirty years ago, if someone had asked me what I thought about manufacturing, I would have said that it was about as interesting as a bowl of Jell-O. Manufacturing was something done in factories, and factories were dirty, noisy places where engineers, cost accountants, and other staid and steady kinds of people spent their working hours purchasing raw materials, controlling inventories, establishing production standards, and supervising hourly workers who, in turn, also had dull, routine jobs. The exciting part of a business, I thought, was not on the factory floor, but in marketing and finance. Advertising, sales promotion, market research, new product development, market segmentation, and pricing were the topics that fascinated me.

I started my career as a salesperson for Union Starch and Refining Corporation. The central administrative and marketing offices were in Columbus, Indiana, hundreds of miles from the industrial refinery. All of us in the marketing department had studied the chemistry of our products—corn starch and corn syrup—but most of us, including the corporate officers, had little understanding of or appreciation for production. I can recall the afternoon that the president of the company, who also happened to be my mentor, told me, "I don't care if our products are made by left-handed gnomes, so long as our commodities are as good as our competitors'."

At the time, that attitude was ubiquitous in the United States. And the results of such disdain proved disastrous for many American industries. Although few, if any, other countries are better endowed with natural resources or technology or have a healthier or better-educated labor force than the United States, a long list of American consumer and industrial goods—autos, window fans, steel, musical instruments, machine tools, televisions, cameras—are having a hard time competing with similar goods made by foreign producers.

But not all Americans are slow to learn. Today there's a dramatic revolution going on in manufacturing, making it the most exciting and dynamic area of business. Such companies as Steelcase, Harley Davidson, Maytag, Hewlett-Packard, John Deere, Merck, Black & Decker, Sperry, Intel, 3M, Burlington, Lincoln Electric, and Johnson Wax have set their sights on being top performers.

Today over 100 American companies have at least one factory that's a world-class producer, able to match any other producer for quality, reliability, and price. General Motors, for example, a mammoth organization with over 500,000 employees and fourteen administrative layers from shop floor to the presidency, set out 10 years ago to develop a new type of truck assembly plant in Shreveport, Louisiana. Unencumbered by traditional management policies, the management team was given the responsibility of developing an efficient assembly plant. It did much more. Today this GM plant is not only recognized for the extraordinary quality and reliability of its trucks, but this factory is also a world leader in safety, productivity, and innovation. Morale is high and so are profits. I've been told that the two places Japanese auto executives want to visit in the U.S. are DisneyWorld and the GM truck plant in Shreveport—a pocket of excellence in the middle of one of the largest and most complex organizations on the face of the earth.

How is it that some producers of pharmaceuticals, welding equipment, motorcyles, computers, and farm machinery have managed in less than 10 years to successfully compete in and lead world markets? How did ordinary producers become extraordinary producers?

The answers to these questions are almost as surprising as the phenomena that raised them in the first place. None of these high-performing firms used quick fixes. All of them viewed reaching the goal of excellence as a long-term, never-ending process that had to involve everyone in the organization—not just managers or supervisors. These world-class manufacturers focus on the same three areas. And the formula for excellence that they use is this:

Total Commitment to Quality
+ Total Commitment to Productivity
+ <u>Total Commitment to the Involvement of People</u>
= Manufacturing Excellence

There is a deep belief in all these firms that there is no trade-off between quality and productivity, and both depend on highly motivated people. Furthermore, like a forest fire that burns hotter the faster it burns, the employees of these firms are motivated by success and work even harder to be even more successful. They keep on raising their standards of excellence.

To maintain their world-class standing all these manufacturers abide by the following rules:

1. *Choose simplicity over complexity.* Striving for simplicity is not the same thing as being simplistic. A simple idea can be elegant. And elegant is the perfect word to describe the breathtakingly simple concepts and ideas used by these firms.

For example, the just-in-time (JIT) concept can be understood by an 8-year-old. If you frequent a large supermarket with a good fruit and vegetable department, you've seen this concept in action. The inventory is always there in sufficient quantity, yet there are no large stockpiles of carrots or peaches in the bins or the back room. Shipments arrive frequently—just in time.

The application of this simple idea to factory size, plant layout, and supplier and worker relations borders on being astounding. Using JIT, Toyota produced 1,500 six-cylinder engines a day with a workforce of 161 on two shifts in 1990. The company doesn't use robots or fancy new equipment; the engines move on simple conveyors and the workpiece movement is regulated by the engine hitting leather flappers—not by computers or laser counters. The rate of production varies with the rate that the finished engines are taken from the line. International comparisons are difficult to make, but one study revealed that a U.S. automaker's plant in Michigan required seven times the space and nearly five times as much labor to produce the same output.

2. *Keep wide perspectives on corporate goals, not narrow ones.* People in all kinds of jobs—shipping clerks, secretaries, production workers, as well as managers—view their jobs in terms of the customer's perception of their product. For example, when a Harley Davidson factory worker was asked what he did for a living, he could have said, "I work in the tool room." But he responded, "I am making the finest motorcycle in the world."

3. *Don't hide problems; make them visible to everyone.* World-class producers *like* to find problems. This might initially sound bizarre, but it makes a lot of sense. Little problems that are swept under the rug eventually create an unsightly lump. Once uncovered, problems can be viewed as opportunities for improvement. The only way to increase customer satisfaction is to continually improve everything associated with the product—shipping, delivery, instruction books, billing, safety—as well as the product itself. And the best way to do that is to keep a sharp eye out for glitches.

The firms that follow this rule find simple but effective ways to chart their progress. Each work area uses tables and graphs to illustrate its performance, and everyone in the plant can look at everyone else's "report card." Every small success is noticed and applauded.

The most fascinating thing to remember is that the formula for excellence used in the manufacturing sector can be applied to almost any organization. A department store, for example, can become world-class by using it, and so can a restaurant, bank, or supermarket. It can also be applied to nonprofit organizations. What's stopping a community from having a world-class school system, police force, or hospital? Why can't this formula be applied to organizations that pick up trash, teach children, care for the sick, and promote public safety? Are we being blocked by our own rigid thinking patterns? Or is the fear of failing or the fear of the unknown keeping our aspirations low?

My first boss was a brilliant and sensitive manager; however, he was absolutely wrong when he said he didn't care who made his products. The men and women in the trenches do count. They count for almost everything. Yes, top managers must make the initial commitment to follow the formula for excellence. But it's up to the factory workers, teachers, nurses, salespeople, clerks, and computer programmers to sustain the drive for excellence.

Case Studies in Excellence

The Tampa Triangle

When you hear the term "Bermuda Triangle," images of danger and mysterious disappearances, no doubt, come to your mind.

The "Tampa Triangle," on the other hand, is neither dangerous nor mysterious. There is nothing occult or supernatural about it. Rather, it is a powerful, simple concept that all of us can use in our daily lives.

The Tampa Electric Company has earned a reputation for being one of the best-managed utilities in the United States. Any way you want to measure its success—in terms of growth, innovation, profitability, customer satisfaction, employee retention, or productivity—it is a leader.

How can it do so well in an industry that's noted for having so many employees who sleepwalk through their jobs?

Recently, I was invited to be the guest speaker at a large banquet for a professional society in Tampa. During the dinner, I turned to a bright-eyed woman at my table and asked her where she worked.

"Tampa Electric," she said.

"Do you like your job?" I asked.

"No," she replied, "I don't like my job." She paused, and then said, "I love my job!"

The next day, when I spoke with a cross section of Tampa Electric employees, I found out that everyone—without exception—was enthusiastic about the company in general and about their own work area in particular. They believed their company was the best, but they were not satisfied. At my workshop, managers from different divisions carried on exchanges with no apparent sense of status. People laughed and teased one another, and yet they seemed passionate about and committed to their own department.

What created this extraordinary work environment?

There is, of course, no simple answer, but one concept that they all knew and apparently used is what I call the "Tampa Triangle."

A triangle has three sides. The ancient Egyptians and Babylonians considered the number three magical. And in everyday life, items used in threes have some special practical characteristics. Why do surveyors and photographers use tripods and not "quadpods?" Why do milking stools have three legs and not four or five or, for that matter, one wide leg?

Three legs provide what scientists call an elegant solution to a problem. A milking stool with one or two legs would not be stable. Even a very wide leg, like a big piece of sawed-off tree trunk, makes for a tippy stool when placed on a barn floor. But three legs, whether on a tripod or a milking stool, create a stable and steady situation. The Great Pyramid is made up of three triangles and it has stood for almost 5,000 years.

The Tampa Triangle has a dynamic equilibrium about it. It provides a foundation for the corporation and a guideline for all human relations in the company. But it can be used by any group involved in any task. Teachers, coaches, supervisors, sales managers—everyone can use this approach to motivate themselves and others. This management triangle has three legs and all three legs are connected. The three legs are

1. Ask for help.
2. Listen empathetically.
3. Enhance self-worth.

Aren't these simple ideas? Are you surprised to find that such simple concepts form the basic foundation for this extraordinary company? Do you feel like Dorothy in *The Wizard of Oz* when she discovered that the Wizard had no mysterious powers?

Don't be fooled by the simplicity of these concepts. It takes an immense amount of work to make the principles behind the Tampa Triangle part of the daily operation of an organization. If this philosophy were easy to implement, everyone would be doing so. It's simple, but not easy.

Leg 1: Ask for help. Think about the effect this concept can have on an organization. What does it say to employees when managers ask for their help? Does it mean that they are weak leaders? That they are lazy? Does it mean that they have lost control? No. When done in an honest and open way, it says something else. A manager who asks for help is sending a message that says, "All of us on this team have a problem, and I need your ideas, unique perceptions, and knowledge to help me deal with this issue." A manager who asks for help is also saying, "I am not a superhero, a computer, or a Mr. Spock; I am a fallible and truth-seeking human being who, like you, is struggling to do the right thing."

When was the last time your superior or boss asked your help—not to take on some extra task, but help that required your creative thinking and experience? When was the last time you asked for help? When you invite someone to help you, aren't you saying to that person, "You are a valuable person, and you have insights and ideas that can help us"? Aren't you telling that person that he or she is not an interchangeable part but, rather, a unique and special person?

Asking employees for help dignifies them and their place in the group. The sense of being needed may be the strongest motivator there is—maybe even stronger than money, sex, or power.

Leg 2: Listen empathetically. What does it mean to listen empathetically? How many people can listen without judging or interjecting their ideas? Empathetic listeners are so rare that most of us are surprised and delighted when we come across a person who listens in this way.

Think of the ideas, thoughts, and suggestions that you could produce if you knew that your embryonic notions would not be met with indifference or, worse, with such typical jeers and derision as "What a stupid idea!" or "We've tried that before."

Could you imagine a work environment in which people try not to just listen to the words, but to sense and understand what that person is experiencing from his or her own particular situation?

Several years ago, one of my college students, Margo Johnson, sat down next to me in the college coffee shop. She pulled out her paper. It was covered with red-inked remarks and corrections.

"Dr. Richardson," she said, "I think you really put students down."

I was aghast. "What do you mean, Margo?" I asked.

"Look—all you've done is point out my mistakes," she replied.

My first impulse was to disagree with her. I wanted to ask her if she knew how much time and effort I had put into grading her paper. Then something clicked. For the first time in many years of teaching, I saw the corrected paper from the student's point of view. She was right.

Now I try to follow a three-point formula in grading papers. First, I tell the student what is good about the paper; second, I indicate how the paper missed the mark; and third, I give specific suggestions for improving the paper and I offer my help if it's needed.

How well do you listen to complaints? How empathetically do you listen to novel ideas or, better yet, how well do you sense unspoken feelings?

Employees at Tampa Electric are self-conscious about listening empathetically. They take workshops on the topic, practice the skill, help one another, and use listening ability as a criterion for performance reviews.

Leg 3: Enhance self-worth. Self-worth has become a pop-psych term. Yet, how we feel about ourselves will influence how we treat others and also how they treat us. And it's important to remember that we can have great self-confidence and yet not really feel good about ourselves.

Rather than building self-confidence and self-worth, many work environments are actually destructive. Rather than enlarge people's psyches, they shrink them. The negative behavior of the boss is emulated by subordinates at work, since this is their model for success, and the employees take this attitude and outlook home and, thereby, infect their family.

Managers at Tampa Electric know that it is their job to develop the people around them; they act as coaches and teachers. Most employees are involved in some form of continuous training. Employees from all levels and departments are selected to take a specially designed leadership course that teaches them how to train others in human relations. In effect, everyone becomes a teacher and a student.

Most firms contend that they encourage employees to make suggestions and to be entrepreneurial. But employees often are made to feel that such behavior is not in their best interests. At Tampa Electric employees are rewarded for trying—even if the project fails. Because of the high level of trust in the company, people speak out freely and often bluntly. People learn that ideas—their ideas—are valued and that no one has the right to put anyone else down. Top managers consistently emphasize every person's dignity.

Long-term employment, continuous learning, and an emphasis on ethical behavior combine to create a positive environment in which employees feel valued, are asked to produce ideas, and are empowered to put those ideas into place. No wonder people like working for Tampa Electric!

Just imagine how our schools, churches, hospitals, government agencies, banks, and business firms would perform, and how the employees of those organizations would feel about their jobs, their teammates, and themselves, if they took the concepts that make up the Tampa Triangle and put them into action.

A Great Place to Work—Not Too Good to Be True

The organization that has taught me the most about effective management, customer satisfaction, and motivation is a British merchandising firm with a curious name—John Lewis Partnership.

John Lewis is a place where people have fun, as well as work hard. How would you like to work for a firm that offers these benefits:

- Market-level salaries plus, on average, an annual cash bonus of 20 percent.
- Noncontributory pension and generous sick-leave plans.
- Four-week vacation each year, which is increased to 5 weeks after 3 years.

- A discount of 25 percent off the retail price of company goods.
- Access to one of the company's four yachts, golf courses, and subsidized vacation camps.
- Subsidized tickets to concerts and plays.
- Subsidized meals at work.
- Access to inexpensive vacation resorts.
- Membership in local clubs that sponsor a variety of activities—from ski trips to yoga lessons—for their members.

High-performing organizations are highly profitable, but the profit almost always derives from having loyal and enthusiastic customers who are served by highly competent and motivated employees. Let's see how John Lewis Partnership operates.

The John Lewis Partnership was formed in 1929 when John Speden Lewis took over a small group of department stores that his family owned in London and radically changed their philosophy and operation. Operating twenty-three department stores and ninety supermarkets in England, Scotland, and Wales, today the company is one of the largest retail merchandising firms in Great Britain, with sales of $4 billion and 30,000 partners.

John Speden Lewis had neither an academic background in business management nor an interest in management theory. He built the company on the values, philosophy, and pragmatic ideas that he developed over his own lifetime. He realized that employees behave as though they own the business if they actually have a stake in the company. And so, he turned his company into a partnership wherein the entire organization belongs to the staff. Here are a few other ideas that set John Lewis Partnership apart from other commercial organizations:

- *"We are never knowingly undersold."* This unconditional customer guarantee, which U.S. merchants have copied, started with John Lewis.

- *"Treat every customer as though you were waiting on your mother."* This policy guides the behavior of the company's salespeople.

- *There is no advertising budget.* It is hard to imagine a modern department store or supermarket without a considerable newspaper or TV advertising budget. John Speden Lewis believes that everyday low prices and total customer satisfaction will persuade customers that there is little need to shop around.

- *All employees are considered the customers' agents, not agents of the producers.* This means that employees should think and act as though they were the paid advocates of the customers they serve.

- *John Lewis Partnership has a written constitution.* This document spells out the rights and obligations of vendors, partners, and customers, and establishes a process of checks and balances that involves partners at all levels in governing the organization.

- *Charitable contributions are important.* The company gives millions of dollars every year to local charities. Usually the money goes to cultural, environmental, and youth center programs.

Although John Lewis Partnership is certainly one of the most humanistic and employee-centered corporations on earth, it is a no-nonsense, results-oriented, cost-conscious organization. The firm's managers don't spout theory, yet their practices are among the same ones being preached by management gurus around the world.

All of John Speden Lewis's ideas are simple. There is nothing abstruse or complicated about them. Because his vision was clear and his goals noble, he was able to establish a foundation on which a high-performing, profitable, innovative, and ethical organization could grow. The cornerstone of his philosophy is this: "The supreme purpose of John Lewis Partnership is simply the happiness of the members."

What does this quote mean to you? Does it mean that customers' preferences are not important? Does it mean that a department store or a supermarket should become a "country club" for its employees? Hardly. What this statement means is that customer satisfaction begins with those who are doing the serving—and that means every single employee.

John Speden Lewis was not a utopian dreamer or a mushy-brained fool. He believed that organizations, no matter how elaborate or simple, have to run on the basis of trust. He believed that most organizations that lack trust become so encumbered with safeguards, rules, audits, and bureaucracy that their progress is impeded.

Seventy years ago, retail employees were one step away from being indentured servants. John Speden Lewis believed that an environment based on fear and coercion would demotivate workers. They would salute and then do the minimal amount of work required to get by. But if you start with the ordinary worker and ask what can be

done to make a job more challenging, creative, and enno-
bling, and then monitor and reward good performance,
there is no limit to an organization's capacity.

Lewis aimed to give all the employees (partners) the
excitement that owners have when they participate in the
business. Real happiness at work, he believed, requires
the sharing of power, knowledge, and profits. Furthermore, real human happiness also requires an environment
in which there are fair dealings at all times and a sustaining concern for ethics and justice. John Speden Lewis
wrote: "Partnership is justice better than justice. It is kindness. Partnership is a matter of facts and not words." His
three basic tenets were

1. *Share profits.* Why should employees give their best
effort? One reason is that they will be compensated for
it. The idea of profit sharing on an equal proportional basis for everyone—from mailroom to boardroom—was a
radical idea in the 1920s. It still is.

Under John Lewis's form of governance, the partners'
bonuses—which have averaged 20 percent of base pay in
recent years—are a major concern. There are no additional bonuses, golden parachutes, or lush perquisites for
top managers.

2. *Share knowledge.* Why do so many organizations hide
information from employees? If we are all in the same
boat together—as managers like to say—why isn't information about operations, costs, performance, results, and
plans for expansion or contraction openly shared with
employees?

Not too many years ago, physicians felt it was necessary to shield patients from bad news. These white lies

made patients feel like children and created a tense atmosphere of distrust. But contemporary physicians tell the whole story truthfully and in plain terms; so do managers at John Lewis Partnership.

One of the major instruments for sharing information within the company is a high-quality weekly magazine called *The Gazette*. It is sold to employees for about a nickel and contains sales figures for every store and every department. Every job opening, appointment, and promotion is published, along with the minutes of major committee meetings.

Probably the most provocative and frequently read part of *The Gazette* is the Letters to the Editor section. Employees are free to write a letter asking any question or challenging any decision. Some are vitriolic; others are analytical; still others, humorous. Here are some sample excerpts:

- Why do London employees get longer lunch periods than employees in smaller cities?
- Are we using recyled paper? I think we have been deceived!
- Why are our squash counters being taken over for storage space?

The appropriate manager must respond to the partner's anonymous letter in the next issue.

3. *Share power.* The third major plank in the John Lewis Partnership platform is an emphasis on sharing power and responsibility. Managers and supervisors at the company are goal-oriented and involved in monitoring results. John Lewis Partnership had its own type of Management by

Objective (MBO) system before Peter Drucker published the concept.

John Lewis Partnership expects managers to be not only accountable to their superiors, but also to those they manage. This is a radical idea. The boss must share information and decision-making authority with the team members.

Store managers are audited by their superiors. Every 6 months the partners of a particular store meet with the regional manager after the store is closed. The store manager does not come to this meeting. There is an open exchange about what is going on and a discussion about how the store manager is leading and managing. This idea was in place 50 years before Tom Peters advocated "management by walking around."

Employees are elected by their peers to sit on all sorts of councils, boards, and operating committees. They have input on expansion decisions, bonus allocations, and changes in disciplinary and benefit policies. Here are some of the ways in which the company encourages the sharing of power:

- Employees help hire other employees. In many cases, new employees are friends or relatives of current employees.

- Employee peer group review and input determine whether a probationary employee gains permanent status.

- Each store has an ombudsman who reports directly to the chairman, not the store manager. If a person has a problem at work—discrimination, harassment, or other conflict—or a personal problem—regarding their career, a drug or other health issue, or even their child—the ombudsman will help the person get counseling or other assistance. These dealings are always confidential.

For decades, John Lewis Partnership has been doing many things that seem modern or even radical today. Most of these practices have come from the logic of treating employees as adults who want to be in a secure, trusting, and ethical yet challenging environment that provides superior service all the time. By focusing on an employee's inherent desire to be productive and part of a winning team, the company has become and remains a great place to work.

Managing With an Open Hand

Have you ever scooped up a handful of dry sand at the beach and then closed your hand around it? All of us who have done this have discovered what at first seems like a paradox.

If you try to hold the sand in your clenched fist, some of the sand slips out of the bottom. If you try to remedy this problem by gripping even tighter, more sand slips through your fingers. The tighter you grip, the less sand you have.

Managers who manage people with an ever-tightening grip often find that employees' enthusiasm diminishes, their willingness to take risks fades, and a vast amount of emotional and mental energy is used to defend their behavior and blame others for mistakes.

Innovation in such an environment is seen as a threat. New ideas, technologies, and methods are resisted because employees see themselves as "interchangeable factors of production" that are "costs to be eliminated" by managers. Why work yourself out of a job, even if it is a bad one? At least it's a job.

The unsought consequences of the tightening-grip approach to management can be seen in multinational corporations and in mom-and-pop shops. Well-run organizations do measure, monitor, and control, but they do so by using goals and standards to inspire and guide people rather than choke them. Monitoring becomes a way for individuals and teams to take self-corrective and creative actions to improve a situation—not to shift blame.

What happens when an organization is managed with an open hand instead of a tight fist? Let's go to Midlothian, Texas, and see.

Midlothian. It sounds like a place that Gulliver might have visited in his travels. This small town of 3,962 people, some 30 miles south of Dallas, is the home of a large concrete firm, Chaparral Steel.

In the early 1970s, the managers of this firm decided to make steel products that were used by their concrete customers. They invited Gordon Forward, who has a Ph.D. in metallurgy and years of experience at a conventional steel firm, to get things started. The founding team developed a revolutionary approach for making quality steel through the use of astute marketing strategies and modern technology and, most important, by unleashing the creative and intellectual energies of all employees.

What happens when management defines each person as a valuable resource to be nurtured rather than as a tool to be used and replaced? What happens when employees understand how passionate and committed management is to their beliefs? What happens when people realize their ideas are needed and will be put into action? What happens when people feel free to experiment, disagree with their bosses, and challenge top management with no fear of punishment? What happens when information is shared and trust and openness characterize all transactions? What happens when profits are shared—and losses, too? What happens when employees own shares in the company and every person's salary is related to performance?

The policies and practices of the Chaparral Steel Company reflect the basic values of Gordon Forward and his team. They believe that every single person has immense intellectual and creative capacity, and that it's management's job to turn this potential energy into kinetic form. Gordon Forward often explains that manufacturing means "to make things by hand." But he has coined a term to capture his philosophy regarding the importance of the *mental* effort behind the manufacturing process—"mentofacturing."

Different and better ways of doing things require the disciplined focus of the human mind. Rather than being limited to the minds of a few managers, Forward's philosophy is built on establishing an environment in which everyone will choose to use his or her mind to improve customer service and reduce costs.

There are thousands of managers around the world who espouse ideas like trust in people, risk-taking, human growth and learning, and having fun at work. Who would ever say they were against such values? But the truth is that most managers pay lip service to these ideas and then walk a different way than they talk. Here are some of the policies that are put into practice at Chaparral:

1. *No-fault absenteeism.* Everyone is expected to come to work. But employees who don't—because they're sick or

because they choose to stay home and watch a ballgame on TV—are paid anyway. But employees know that they let their team down when they are absent. Daily absenteeism is less than 1 percent.

2. *All employees are salaried.* Everyone—night janitors, production workers, secretaries, supervisors—receives a monthly salary. There are no time clocks. Two-thirds of the employees own Chaparral stock, and bonuses average 8 percent of gross profits.

3. *No two people get the same salary.* Each employee's individualized salary is reviewed and adjusted on the date of his or her anniversary of employment. There is no standard adjustment. Performance reviews by superiors as well as the employee's own evaluations are factored into pay increases.

4. *The environment is informal, democratic, and not bureaucratic.* Face-to-face communication replaces most memos and reports. There are no executive dining rooms. The boardroom is in the same building as the training classrooms. The employee classrooms have better equipment and are better appointed than the boardrooms. Locker rooms and executive offices are also in the same building.

5. *Education is continuous.* Every employee receives 120 hours of training per year—and they are paid a small premium for participation in the training. "Sabbaticals"—fully paid, short leaves—are given each year to every supervisor so they can attend a university course, visit a steel

plant abroad, or work in a customer's plant for a few weeks.

6. *Problems are sought out.* The whole factory is viewed as a laboratory. This means that engineers, supervisors, and factory workers can experiment directly on the production process. Research and innovation are linked. Everyone—not just design engineers—can participate in innovation.

7. *There are no job descriptions.* The labor force is flexible and can do many jobs. Employees continue to learn how to do their jobs better or may also learn other jobs. There are only three layers separating a factory worker from the executive committee.

8. *Chaparral prides itself on being known as a great place to work.* Although jobs are demanding and there is continuous pressure to reduce costs and improve processes, employees often say they love working at Chaparral because it's fun. The turnover rate is low—about 4 percent per year.

9. *Employee selection is a serious process.* Since Chaparral has such a good reputation, there are often hundreds of applicants for each vacancy. The human resources department screens potential employees through testing and interviews. Those who pass (one out of eight) meet with a work team for several hours. The applicants' work histories, attitudes, and human relations skills are assessed. And every new hire is required to participate in a 1-week orientation program. Filling a vacancy may take 4-6 weeks.

10. *Self-managed work teams are used.* Every employee belongs to a team that is responsible for managing itself. As part of their team, each employee is expected to devise ways to improve productivity.

What has happened to this upstart steel company, which in 1975 set as its goal to be the world's lowest-cost producer of high-quality construction- and industrial-grade steel products?

Today it is the twelfth-largest steel producer in the United States, with sales of around $500 million. Its customers consider it to be one of the easiest steel companies to do business with because it delivers on time and can make adjustments to meet end-users' needs. It is also the world's lowest-cost producer in terms of labor hours per ton of steel. The average labor productivity per ton of steel in the United States is 3.6 person-hours per ton. Chaparral takes only 1.4 person-hours per ton—which beats all competitors, even those in Japan and Korea.

Chaparral is not a traditional steel firm. It is a highly capital-intensive factory. The workers melt scrap metal (mostly automobiles) and convert this steel into rods, bars, and other shapes. The whole process is continuous; a scrap auto can be processed into finished products and shipped in under 3 hours.

In 1984 *Fortune* magazine picked Chaparral Steel as one of the best managed factories in America. Tom Peters named Gordon Forward, the firm's president, Executive of the Year in 1987. And in 1989 Chaparral was awarded the Japanese Industrial Standard Award for Quality—the only U.S. steel firm to have this honor.

Success is usually the result of many factors. Chaparral did not invent the minimill concept or much of the technology it uses. The company benefits from a fine location and it knows how to stay close to its customers. It has a clear vision. Since the company's inception, management has aspired to dominate the markets it chose to serve. All these factors are important, but Gordon Forward and his staff would agree that what is unique about their company is its commitment to letting all 960 employees share in the pride and joy of being part of a winning team that aims to be second to none.

An open hand carries more sand than a clenched fist.

Learning From Those Who Help Themselves

Traditional profit-making businesses don't have a monopoly on bright ideas and innovative management. Sometimes we can learn the most from organizations that weren't founded as businesses at all. In fact, if an honor for the single most effective organization were to be given today, I would vote for Alcoholics Anonymous.

A.A., as the organization is commonlly called, was started in 1934 by Bob Smith, a medical doctor, and Bill Wilson, a stockbroker. These men had two things in common: First, they were addicted to alcohol; second, they believed that there was a way out of their miserable existence and they were willing to commit their lives to this quest.

They came up with an idea that, like all great ideas, was simple. Powerfully simple. Deceptively simple. They believed that alcoholism was a disease—like diabetes—that could be dealt with, but not cured.

The basic philosophy of A.A. has changed very little since Bill Wilson articulated the twelve steps that can lead alchoholics to recovery. A small group of anonymous people provide support, understanding, discipline, and affirmation for those who want to stop drinking. Individuals are not allowed to blame others, but are helped to change bad behaviors and take responsibility for their own lives. Today there are over 2 million members who have formed more than 96,000 groups in 114 countries.

This organization is growing at an estimated 4 percent annual rate. Millions of people have gone through the A.A. program and are now living sober and productive lives.

A.A. was not developed by men who studied management or applied psychology. Rather, their policies, strategies, organizational principles, and traditions are based on pragmatic discoveries. Most A.A. members are not interested in the theory of why their programs work any more than most of us wonder or care how a microwave oven works. Nonetheless, there are at least five powerful, pragmatic principles—all of which can be used in any organization—at work in A.A. It would be hard to find better principles than these in any management textbook.

1. *Focus on one thing and don't take your eyes off it.* A.A. exists for one purpose: To help people who want to be helped to stay sober a day at a time. This organization has clearly identified a single mission. Look at all the things A.A. chooses not to be. It is not a church. It is not a welfare society. It is not a school, a hospital, or a social club. In marketing terms, it has only a single product and it has no penchant to add to the product line.

How many organizations have lost their way by losing sight of their purpose? Most mainline churches are declining while other organizations that answer the spiritual and personal needs of individuals are flourishing. Empty pews and filled counseling offices. Why is this?

Most universities in the United States have lost their way. The idea that the university exists to improve the knowledge, skills, and attitudes of students may be given lip service, but an impartial visitor from another planet who visited our campuses would immediately see a great disparity between intentions and results.

Why doesn't a McDonald's restaurant have vending machines or sell candy or gum at the check-out counter? McDonald's focuses on the significant few things that they have learned to do brilliantly—deliver food of a consistent quality in a short time at reasonable prices.

An organization does not always have to stay with the same focus. Indeed, doing so can be suicidal. But leaders must be clear about whom they choose to serve and their competitive advantage. How can you play your strength unless you know what it is?

2. *Maintain a lean central administration.* A.A. has only 110 full-time employees in its central office, and 90 of these are involved in clerical functions. More than 2 million members and so few managers!

This obviously means that individual A.A. groups are basically self-directed. This works in practice because the members share a common purpose, traditions, and rituals. Most organizations are over-managed and over-led. Not A.A. And like A.A., McDonald's, Wal-Mart, and other high-performing organizations have small central offices and a lean staff.

3. *Rotate leadership.* One reason traditionally managed organizations have so many layers of management is that

each manager can only direct, evaluate, and control a limited number of people. But if you change some basic assumptions, you can take different approaches.

What if we assumed that most people had the capacity to direct themselves? What if people could come together voluntarily and identify for themselves what tasks and priorities needed to be addressed? Could leadership come out of the work group? Could leaders feel accountable and responsible not only to the boss but also to the group?

A.A. functions so well because everyone is looked upon as a responsible adult who initiates, directs, and controls his or her own life, and everyone can use their talents in leading and managing A.A. groups. In fact, rotating leadership is one of the cardinal principles of A.A. groups.

How could this idea be applied in industry? Could it work? Frito-Lay is a good example of how rotating leadership can work. Employees on the factory floor work in self-directed groups. There are clear rules from the central administration, but these groups are empowered to select their own leaders, decide how they will improve quality, reduce costs, and handle disciplinary problems.

How do people feel when they are in an environment where they are treated like ambitious, intellectual adults? How do you think these employees feel when their own ideas are put into operation? Both worker satisfaction and production are high at Frito-Lay.

4. *Act your way to good thinking, don't think your way to good acting.* Do actions follow thoughts, or do thoughts follow actions? This is a provocative question.

But A.A. is clear about one thing: Individuals who want to live sober, productive lives need to do more than wish, theorize, and think. They must stop drinking. By changing behaviors, which is often very difficult to do, millions of people have changed their attitudes, thoughts, and feelings about themselves and others.

In practical terms, there is a lesson here not only for people battling addictions, but also for leaders of any organization. Managers must be clear about the specific behaviors they expect an employee to change—not being tardy, not giving bad looks, or not saying put-downs.

5. *Develop self-esteem and trust.* A.A. groups start their meetings on time, and they don't encourage debates, sermons, whining, self-pity, or ego-trips. This is not an association filled with lots of "shoulds" or "ought to's." A.A believes that to err is human.

How would you like to be a member of a group that does not expect perfection—just your best effort with no excuses attached?

Does A.A. actually deliver what it has set out to do? Few institutions, if any, have had a more permanent and positive impact on human lives. For over 50 years A.A. has served its members well. Nearly 60 percent of those who attend meetings for one year remain in A.A. This is amazing. Furthermore, many people who attend A.A. meetings for some period of time drop out when they feel they no longer need group support. That means that the actual number of people who are living more productive lives because of A.A.'s self-help program is probably several million.

Let's put the case for A.A.'s effectiveness more dramatically. What percentage of criminals do you think change their behavior after serving a jail sentence? Do you know of any leadership or weight-reduction program in which six out of ten participants have a provable and permanent change in their behavior?

A.A. gets results. But results aren't everything; after all, Mussolini made the trains run on time and the Pharaohs created the pyramids. A.A. is one of the most effective organizations in the world not only because it produces results but also because it restores a sense of self-worth and personal dignity to people who are suffering. One A.A. member wrote, "I came to A.A. to save my ass—then I discovered it was attached to my soul."

All of us need to be reminded that how we act out our lives at work, at home, at play, and in our other daily transactions will affect our souls. The good news is that we need not change others, only ourselves, to feel more fully human. Yet, by giving to others what we crave for ourselves—love, respect, and patience—we not only make our own souls sing, but we increase the probability that we will get back what we give.

School Power

I have always been fascinated by success stories. As a 10-year-old, I would listen to a radio personality who liked to relate stories of people who had overcome tremendous barriers to attain their goals. Later, as a teenager, I kept a scrapbook of unusual athletic teams. My favorite was the story of how the basketball team from Hebron High School, which had only 75 students, won the Division One Illinois State Basketball Tournament. As an adult, I became intrigued with organizations that made dramatic reversals. Stories about orchestras, hospitals, manufacturing plants, and retail stores that were able to move from last place to the winner's circle became new scrapbook material for me. One of the most impressive reversal stories I know involves a group of public schools serving inner-city children.

There are some high-performing public schools in the United States. But a vast number of public schools across the country do not deliver what parents want. The additional government resources allocated to schools over the last 30 years have probably improved education, yet few people connected with public education are satisfied with either the process or the results.

Minority children from economically deprived backgrounds have a particularly hard time making it in public school. These children generally start off behind on the first day of school, and most continue to lag behind the national average in academic performance.

Nearly 50 percent of minority students in large cities never finish high school. For a vast proportion of these undereducated people, access to job opportunities is blocked. They will never get on the social and economic escalators that the majority of mainstream Americans take for granted. The failure to educate so many potentially able human minds results in the alienation of millions of individuals and represents a terrible loss to society.

In 1967, James P. Comer, a professor of child psychology and director of the School Development Program at Yale University, and some of his associates were motivated to do something about this situation.

Comer, who does not have a background in management, was able to gather valuable insights from his own experiences as a black child growing up in East Chicago, Indiana.

Why, he wondered, had he been so successful in school? The answer is found in the values he learned at home and in his community. His parents—particularly his mother—had great respect for teaching and learning. She taught him appropriate social skills and affirmed his good work at school. She knew the school administrators and was aware of his day-to-day activities.

Comer reasoned that many impoverished children had learned different values at home and were deficient in mainstream social skills. No matter how progressive their curriculum changes or how advanced their technology, schools—teachers and administrators—were not equipped to address the basic problems that these students faced.

Using a novel management approach, Comer and his associates focused on not just trying to solve individual problems—low math scores, for example—but on ferreting out factors that were inhibiting learning. The children Comer wanted to help came to elementary school with underdeveloped social skills—skills that are desperately needed to perform in any school environment.

These children were smart enough. There was nothing wrong with their brains. They had learned skills and behaviors that served them well in their households, on the streets, and at the playground. But the same kinds of behaviors that children need to survive in hostile environments can cause friction in school. Teachers and principals often have problems disciplining these children. Teachers' expectations are low, and school officials tend to rely on threats, coercion, and punishments to keep the children in line. This leads to a cycle of low expectations, bad behavior, coercion, low performance, parental distrust, and low faculty morale.

Comer realized that parents, staff, teachers, students, and the community really have the same mission. Everyone wants children to learn, to grow in self-confidence, and to find a path to success. But if everyone wants high performance in public schools, why is there such low performance? Of course, the easiest thing to do is to blame someone. Teachers blame administrators, parents, or television. Parents blame teachers or administrators. Administrators blame university preparatory programs, the school board, teachers, or parents.

How unproductive! It is no wonder that many schools are filled with burned-out teachers, frustrated administrators, unhappy parents, and low-performing children.

To break the cycle, James Comer developed a different way of planning, organizing, and motivating staff, students, and parents. The system makes use of three interacting subsystems.

1. *A Governance and Management Team.* In traditional school systems, teachers have some control in the classroom, but the principal is in charge. In Comer's system, parents, teachers, administrators, and support staff become active advisors to the principal. This team discusses current problems and establishes priorities on both social and academic issues. The basic concern is what can all the team members do to make a better place for students to learn? How can the team get the resources it needs or knock down the barriers that stand in its way?

2. *A Mental Health Support Staff Team.* Made up of teachers, parents, and administrators, this team also features professional child development personnel, including a social worker, a special education teacher, a child psychologist, and a nurse. This team handles individual student behavior problems and works on preventing problems. The members initiate new ventures and procedures for establishing a nonthreatening environment in which students can be successful.

3. *The Parents Program.* Parents work in the cafeteria, in the classroom as teachers' aides, and in the library. They attend school functions and interact with students and faculty. Parents are coached in child development theory and practice. With the help of twenty to thirty parents, teachers plan and implement social activities to meet the goals of the steering committee.

In 1969, when this program was initiated in New Haven, Connecticut, the pilot school selected ranked thirty-two out of thirty-three schools on standardized achievement tests. By the time they reached fourth grade, students in this school were 19 months *below* their level in mathematics and reading. There were high levels of absenteeism and serious disciplinary problems in the school.

By 1984, students in the New Haven pilot school were tied for third place in academic achievement in the city. Students on average were 7 months *above* grade level. The students consistently ranked first or second in attendance, and the teachers held the best attendance record in the city. There have been no major disciplinary problems reported in the last ten years. Another problem school in New Haven began this same program in 1977 and, in less than 10 years, moved in rank up to fourth.

Both schools are 99 percent black, and 90 percent of the students come from families that are economically classified as being either at or near the poverty level.

What is going on in these schools? Parents are involved in "Welcome Back to School" dinners, orientation for new students, and graduation celebrations, and they recruit other parents to participate. Parents help tutor children and teach them social skills: personal hygiene, how to write thank-you notes, taking messages on the phone, working in groups, listening to others, and getting along with classmates. Parents as well as teachers model good behavior for these children to follow. The children are able to observe adults who respect learning and care about them as individuals.

Before the program was introduced, an average of fifteen to twenty parents attended school events. With the program in place, parent attendance has increased to as many as 400 adults at an evening function. This is fantastic, considering that the school only enrolls 300 students! Some parents are so energized by their contact with the school that they themselves go back to school. The Comer program creates a positive, affirming environment for both students and parents.

Can this approach be replicated? Will it work outside New Haven and where Comer and his associates are not present?

In fact, the same approach was implemented at schools in Prince George's County, Maryland, and Bentor Harbon, Michigan, in the 1980s. These schools primarily served impoverished minority children. The results in Maryland and Michigan were similar to those of the two schools in New Haven.

The Comer concept has spread. Over fifty schools around the country are using this technique. Here are five lessons that managers of all types of organizations can learn from Comer's educational approach:

1. *Fix the system, not the symptom.* When we find low-performing factories or hospitals, the first step is to search for the underlying cause. Coercion and rewards may help increase productivity in the short run, but these approaches usually cover up the real problem.

2. *Don't blame.* James Comer doesn't blame the teachers, students, or administrators for poor performance. He did not blame parents or television or a decline in the work ethic. Instead, Comer employed a diagnostic approach to analyze the situation. He realized that the six-year-old children he wanted to help were not stupid or lazy. Their parents and the others who nurtured them were not mean or selfish. There are no bad guys—but there are inappropriate environments.

3. *Put all the oars in the water and pull in the same direction.* How would a rowing team perform if some people were back-paddling, some were barely pulling, and some had their oars out of the water all together? Confusion, name-calling, and low morale would be expected. And needless to say, the team wouldn't travel very far.

The basic genius of Comer's approach is that he develops teams. Team members want the same thing: an environment that will improve the self-confidence and competence of the children. Parents, teachers, administrators, and staff believe in what they're doing and choose to give their best effort because they believe their goal is a worthy one. They know the task before them is hard. They know that others have given up or are coasting along. But they also know that they have been asked to help do something that is important.

4. *Everyone can be a creative thinker and a hands-on worker.* Although a parent may not have a high-school diploma, it does not mean that he or she is not intelligent. In Comer's management system, parents with modest educations work with psychiatrists and professional educators. Parents contribute ideas, share in decision-making, and participate in programs. They also demonstrate what it is to be a servant leader by working in classrooms, libraries, and cafeterias. Parents model good behavior and their behavior speaks louder than a sermon.

5. *Leadership exists at all levels and in all places.* There is more to the Comer plan than putting parents on teams and committees. Leadership is the leaven that lifts these schools' performance.

Principals who want to try this approach must have self-confidence and courage. They must not give up responsibility, but they do have to share power. This is not easy. Teachers and staff workers lead because of their expertise or because their arguments and insights are so good that others choose to follow. Parents lead by sharing their own special experiences and knowledge and developing activities and programs.

How do you get extraordinary results with ordinary people? The answer seems to be the same whether you examine a successful utility company, department store chain, factory, nonprofit organization, or school.

8

Managing by Metaphor

We are coming to the end of our journey. I hope that you've found it enjoyable and meaningful.

Along the way we stopped off at places that may have surprised you, places like Easter Island, Salisbury Cathedral, Stonehenge, and the top of the Sears Tower. We also met some fascinating people—Cardini the magician, Perry Gresham, Albert Einstein. And all the while we explored some provocative concepts—management metaphors that encapsulate a great store of information.

Now here's a chance to see if these metaphors stick in your memory and can be readily retrieved. Read the following questions. How many can you answer?

- What is the +10 Percent Principle? Can you explain it to a fifth-grader? Is it a literal concept or a metaphor? What does it mean to you? What can it mean to a group or team? How might this principle be used to plan, organize, and motivate a girls' softball team, a church's outreach program, or a corporate department?

239

- Can you draw the pictogram for the Chinese eye? Why does it look the way it does? Can computers "see" in this way? How have you used this skill?

- Who was Percival Lowell? What did he see when he was looking through a telescope at Mars? Have you ever had an experience in which you saw something because you believed it to be the case? Do we see because we believe, or do we believe because we see? How do you look at people? Can you see great capacities in so-called average people?

- Do you recall the story of the king who wanted to see if newborns kept in isolation would speak their mother tongue when they began to talk? How did the test come out? What does this story mean for children? For adults? Do you need love and affirmation? Is the workplace an appropriate place to fill this need?

- Why doesn't Salisbury Cathedral's 400-foot tower fall down? Are the foundations visible? How does this relate to the history of the Jewish people or to any successful organization?

- How did the ancient people of Easter Island lift their massive stone figures without the use of modern machines? How did Thor Heyerdahl find this out? What does his experience teach us?

- Everyone knows what a lever is, but what's a listening lever? Do Japanese manufacturers use it? Does your company? Your church? Your school? Your mate? Do you?

- How does the root system of a redwood tree differ from that of most other trees? How have they been able to stand for so long? What does this mean to you as a person? As a leader? As a member of a team?

- Can leadership come from children? Elderly people? People with no titles or formal degrees? Give some examples from the preceding chapters. Can you think of examples from your own life?

- Why did the beavers that the team of naturalists studied die? What does this story say about your problem-solving ability? Why are so many organizations reluctant to change?

- What is a one-flavor manager? Can you think of any organizations that have policies that hassle you? What about your children's school or your own company?

You're no doubt surprised at the number of metaphors you were able to recall, and the degree of detail you remembered. Now what do you do with these ideas? Use them to transform your schools, hospitals, banks, stores, plants, hotels, travel agencies, and teams from pedestrian to exceptional organizations. Once you learn to manage by metaphor, you can encourage and attain outstanding performance.

A good friend of mine, Don McDowell, a Methodist minister, tells a story about a man watching a monarch butterfly break out of its cocoon. The beautiful large wings unfolded and the butterfly struggled to get free. But one thin strand attached to the cocoon seemed to be holding it back. Wanting to help the butterfly, the man snipped the strand with a pair of scissors. But rather than flying upward, the butterfly toppled over, shriveled up, and died. The strand that the man had cut was making the butterfly fight hard for its freedom, and that struggle was needed to force blood into the insect's vital organs. Without the necessary struggle, this magnificent butterfly could not survive.

Likewise, developing a high-performance organization takes immense effort. But the process doesn't have to be painful. Think about your own experiences. Were you ever part of a cast that put on a difficult play and did it well? Have you ever been part of an orchestra, scout troup, or charitable committee that worked extremely hard and succeeded? If so, there's probably a smile crossing your face at the happy recollection. How many times in our lives have we been part of a group that did something especially well?

The struggle is well worth it and, as we now know, we need not accomplish a superhuman task or make a gargantuan effort to stand out. After all, the difference between the ordinary and the extraordinary is quite small—just 10 percent more.

Bibliography

Geisel, Theodore (Dr. Seuss). *Horton Hears a Who.* New York: Random House Books for Young Readers, 1954.

Kramer, Jerry, and Dick Schaap. *Instant Replay.* Evanston, IL: Holtzman Press, 1981.

Levering, Robert, and Milton Moskowitz. *The One Hundred Best Companies to Work for in America.* New York: Doubleday, 1993.

Peters, Tom J., and Nancy K. Austin. *A Passion for Excellence.* New York: Warner Books, 1989.

Piper, Watty. *The Little Engine That Could.* New York: Putnam Publishing Group, 1978.

Theroux, Paul. *Riding the Iron Rooster: By Train Through China.* New York: Ivy Books, 1989.